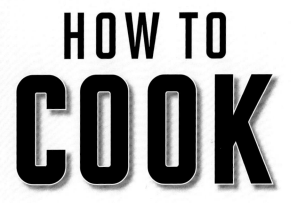

HOW TO
COOK

Clarkson Potter/Publishers
NEW YORK

HUGH ACHESON

HOW TO COOK

**Building Blocks and
100 Simple Recipes
for a Lifetime of Meals**

01 A LIST FOR A FUTURE GENERATION ••••• ➤ page 6

02 WHAT THIS BOOK IS ALL ABOUT ••••• ➤ page 7

03 WHAT IS GOOD FOOD? ••••• ➤ page 9

04 HOW YOU SHOULD SHOP ••••• ➤ page 9

05 COMPLEMENTARY FLAVORS ••••• ➤ page 11

06 HERBS, SPICES, SALT + HOW TO USE THEM ••••• ➤ page 15

07 WHAT YOU NEED IN YOUR KITCHEN ••••• ➤ page 17

08 USING A KNIFE ••••• ➤ page 18

CONTENTS

09 **THE BUILDING BLOCKS** ••••• ➤ page 20

10 **RECIPES** ••••• ➤ page 88

11 ACKNOWLEDGMENTS ••••• ➤ page 219

12 INDEX ••••• ➤ page 220

A LIST FOR A FUTURE GENERATION

Learn how to cook
for yourself.

Wash your hands often.

Don't double-dip, but
do taste as you cook.

Drink lots of water.

Be grateful for the
food in front of you.

Be proud to cook
family recipes.

Adapt leftovers
to new uses.

Buy in season . . .
it is less expensive.

Related: The most
expensive thing is often
not the best thing.

There is nothing wrong
with canned beans.

Don't grocery shop
while hungry.

Clean the outsides
of pots and pans.

Try new things.

Fast food is fine,
but once in a while.

No one has loving
memories of a meal
of pizza pockets.

Salt is a flavor enhancer.
So is MSG. Ain't nothing
wrong with either, in
moderation.

Avoid plastic and
disposables. Compost.
Recycle diligently.

Yes, you can
probably pickle it.

Be nice to farmers,
teachers, postal workers,
and grocery store
clerks. Actually, just
be nice to everyone.

Tip well.

If there is trash on the
ground, pick it up.

Feed your friends
and family. Feed kind
strangers. Realize
the power of giving
nourishment.

WHAT THIS BOOK IS ALL ABOUT

My daughters, Beatrice and Clementine, are well into their teens. I don't think of myself as an overbearing parent, but I wrote that list for them sooner than I want to admit. Growing up the kids of a professional chef, they have been surrounded by good food their whole lives; when I think about them leaving home and living on their own, I want them to feel that they should still be surrounded by good food. I don't expect them to cook like I do, but I do want to make sure they have the basics to be able to feed themselves, their friends, and eventually their own loved ones good, delicious, simple meals. And so I wrote this book, so that you can, too, whether you're leaving home as a teenager, or making your own home, or starting your own family.

What follows is a really simple concept. There are a few ways to cook. One is to read recipes and stress about following them to the letter. Another is to dive into a kitchen and absorb everything, until you can make a bisque, brioche, or baked ziti without ever opening a cookbook.

What I think is the most approachable way to go about it is somewhere in the middle. There should be some very basic things that you know how to make almost from memory. I'm talking about a classic vinaigrette that you can use to dress salads, but also tweak to use as a sauce for roasted vegetables or meats or fish. Or how to cook pasta. Or a perfect grilled cheese, or how to roast a chicken or stir together a simple, flavor-packed herb sauce you can put on anything. Don't worry, there are no tests; you don't really have to memorize any recipes. But I want you to get comfortable making these very basic things, so that you can tweak them, add to or subtract from them, or mix and match them with stuff you have in your fridge, so you can make a meal anytime. Envision a Lego set of cooking skills; once you have those building blocks at hand, cooking becomes a skill you have forever.

So the first part of this book is dedicated to twenty-five building blocks that will anchor your world of cooking and give you the ability to build a system of nourishment. As a professional cook, I rely on core ideas of food to create dishes and menus, and there is no reason you shouldn't do the same.

I've chosen the recipes for the building blocks not just because they're great to make and eat and are flexible in how you use them, but also because in learning to make them, you will learn techniques you can apply to other foods. Learning how to sear a steak, for instance, will give you the same tools you need for searing pork chops or chicken breasts; roasting broccoli will teach you how to roast cauliflower or asparagus.

After those initial building blocks, there are seventy-five more recipes for you to use your new skills . . . or to use the leftovers of what you've already made. In fact, you might want to make some of the building blocks on a Saturday or Sunday afternoon and keep them in your fridge to cook with through the week. I want you to think of leftovers not as "leftovers," but as great ingredients that you can turn into new meals. And with that, you'll be able to cook anytime, forever.

That's me

My daughter, Beatrice

Photo taken by my other daughter, Clementine

WHAT IS GOOD FOOD?

Good food should make you happy to prepare and to eat. Good food powers you and makes you feel lofty and strong. Think of it as a soundtrack to your life.

Flavorwise, good food has strong natural flavor enhanced by salt, punchy nuance, subtle or strong tartness to balance sweetness or richness. It has textures that makes us happy, whether that be the silkiness of perfectly cooked salmon, or the crunch of a simple slaw, or, even better, both of those things together. Good food nourishes us and leaves us content.

I want to show you how to create good food without it being a hassle—without you having to open up a cookbook or download a recipe every time. There will be time involved, yes, and some skill. I'm not promising you a book full of five-minute meals that you will forget about faster than it took you to throw together. But what I will promise you is that cooking good, simple food is time well spent, and the skills you'll learn to do it are skills you'll love having for life.

HOW YOU SHOULD SHOP

Before we cook, we need to shop. We'll get into the tools you should have in your kitchen later, but let's start with the food. And as with everything in cooking, it starts with a list.

I always make lists before I shop, and as a chef, I make lists before I cook—of what to do first, next, and last. You know what a recipe is? It's a list. Lists keep you focused and organized, and keep away distractions.

And speaking of distractions . . . when you walk into the grocery store, just a regular grocery store—not some fancy food palace that makes you feel more economically challenged than normal—you get a cart. If you have a choice, get the smaller one, or even a basket, because the big one is way too large for the way I want you to shop. Studies show that the large carts make you buy up to 40 percent more stuff, by design. I want you to shop like you could be going home on the bus, or driving a tiny car, or riding your bike, which is to say, I want you to buy what you will eat, outside of staples in your larder, within a few days or a week of purchase.

The design of grocery stores is also meant to lure you into buying a lot. The areas outside the center aisles are the areas I tend to stick to, and those areas are usually where the fresh, unprocessed foods are to be found. Produce, deli, butcher, and seafood, then stuff, and stuff, and more stuff, and then dairy. The dairy area, holding the essentials of milk and eggs, is put in the way back corner to make you journey through temptation to get there.

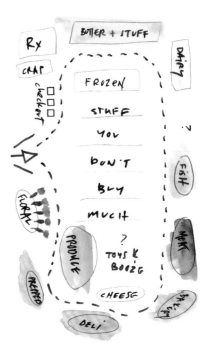

Your choices along the way will make you either the leader of your excursion or a lab rat in a maze of consumerism. Breaking away from how *they* think you will shop is key. In my grocery store, a big-box Kroger in Athens, Georgia, the entrance spills you directly into a floral section, so I bustle past that and am in produce in a matter of steps, the place that I will spend most of my time. It is August, so corn, tomatoes, peaches, green beans, summer squash, melons, and potatoes are relatively local, in good supply, and because of their high seasonality, somewhat inexpensive. Apples, lettuces, cherries, and asparagus are definitely not, so those will not enter my basket, because buying them out of season means they won't be as good, *and* they will cost more, and that doesn't really add up for me. I pick up some tomatoes, four peaches, three summer squash, a small watermelon, and some green beans. I have some basil in a planter at home that will help those ingredients (and if you don't have a planter, but like basil, sure, go pick up some basil).

I move into the deli area, which has a really good cheese selection, but shopping for something as expensive as great cheese needs to be done smartly. There is always a small area of cheeses marked down, with small cuts, and I find some Stilton for a lark. There's a tub of burrata, that soft luxurious cousin of fresh mozzarella, that has a high perishability and is often on sale, and it is . . . at half the cost of the normal price. It will go great with the tomatoes, and I will save the Stilton for a cracker snack.

At this point I have looked in my small pocket notebook in which I store a running inventory of things I need to use that are already in my kitchen. It's sort of the opposite of a shopping list, but the function is the same. Instead of writing down what I need to get, I also write down what I have at home that I want to use, and then I go to the store and find matches for those things. If I've got a pork shoulder, I figure I'm going to cook it for hours and hours until super tender, and then at the store I can decide that I'll use it to make a Korean-style meal. So I'll get lettuce to wrap up the cooked pork, I'll get cucumbers, and at home I have kimchi and some miso. I have rice at home, so don't need that, but I will need ginger and scallions, so a U-turn to the produce section will carve out the rest of that meal.

It may seem like a lot of work to write a shopping list this way, and you don't have to do exactly as I do. But you will find, as you cook more and more, that it can become natural, as you have more and more things you can make without consulting recipes—as you build up the blocks you'll find in this book.

The middle of the store is where the dry goods live, and I make some quick forays to grab things on my shopping list. I buy cider vinegar, some on-sale olive oil, some kosher salt, some spaghetti, and some dried navy beans. I will get spices at the Indian grocery store on Baxter, as they are a quarter of the price and much fresher. I will get dried chiles, tortillas, and some ground pork at the Mexican market because the costs are much lower and the people there are super. The coffee I will get from a shop in town because they roast their own beans and they are nice. Vegetables, other than basics, come from the farmers' market, which is great and operates on Wednesday and Saturday.

I like to shop like this as it gives food the respect it deserves, and I get to spread my money around to different businesses, and I get to support people I like. I recommend it, but I'm not a zealot, and you don't have to be either. Just do what works for you.

COMPLEMENTARY FLAVORS

I get asked all the time, "but what *goes* with that?" Certain foods have long-term friends, a reminder that kinship is always solid ground to stand on. Sliced summer tomatoes only become tastier with basil and shaved sweet onion. Roasted lamb loves mint and chiles. Sometimes there are stranger natural bonds that balance extremes, something I wish would happen more in the human world, like fiery chiles on super sweet mango, or briny olives and tart oranges. But it's not like there is a secret guidebook chefs turn to when they are making dishes for perfect flavor pairings. So let me try to explain by an example.

If I have a couple of summer squash, I begin to move the cogs of my brain in unison with the wants of my stomach. I think about cutting them in thick slices to cook briefly on one side in a good amount of olive oil over pretty high heat. I think about mint,

and lemon zest, and some chile flakes, and some vinaigrette to give us brightness, acidity, and a punch of heat. I figure all that will make a pretty delicious, balanced meal with some protein, maybe just some roasted chicken thighs or a piece of salmon.

SUMMER SQUASH, LEMON, MINT, FETA, VINAIGRETTE

How did I come up with that just like that? Well, thirty years of cooking helps. But you don't have to wait that long. I would start you with a couple of directions. First is know what you like. When you eat food you like, take a second to think about what's in it, what flavors you're tasting that you like together, and start to just keep a mental index of those combinations. Know that if you taste zucchini with mint, lemon zest, and chile flakes together and like it, you can always take your own zucchini and combine it with mint, lemon zest, and chile flakes. Even if you don't make it the same way or get the same dish, you still know that's a combination of flavors you like.

The other thing is, think about breaking those foods down into their component experiences. The zucchini, when roasted with olive oil, is sort of sweet, and rich from the oil. The mint has a fresh flavor. Lemon zest does, too. Chile packs heat. What's missing? In my mind, saltiness and tanginess and richness all go with something sweet and fresh. So I added the vinaigrette. But you could add feta cheese and buttermilk. I could have added Parmesan and lemon juice instead. I could have added ham and sour cream. Any of these would have given me a great mix of the different tastes—salty, sweet, sour, rich. Do what feels good to you, and use what you have. If matching octopus and chocolate is a flavor affinity you think will be great, try it . . . just know that you'll be wrong in that case.

Chart your taste

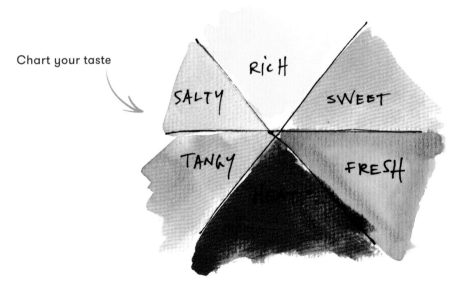

RICH
SALTY
SWEET
TANGY
FRESH

HERBS, SPICES, SALT, AND HOW TO USE THEM

Spices and herbs are sometimes the most overrated and underrated things in the world of food. I say that because some people think the secret to every dish is, well, the "secret herbs and spices." That's usually not true—plenty of great food is just the result of good cooking knowledge and practice, not magic spice blends. But spices and herbs do pack a lot of flavor, so you should know how to use them.

Spices are aromatic seeds, barks, fruits, or flowers. Their flavor lies mostly in the natural oils that they contain, which will dissipate over time. Spices can add a lot to food and sometimes you are aware of a flavor but cannot quite put your finger on it. Pho broth, the clear elixir of Vietnam, is pungent with star anise; pumpkin pie harnesses cloves and nutmeg to give it that autumnal vibe; chai has a bracing backbone of cardamom; gin is only gin because of a steeping of juniper berries. This is all to say that spice can add a lot to food. Buy them in quantities you will use within six months.

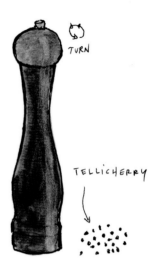

TURN

TELLICHERRY

Your most important spice is pepper for your pepper grinder. It will be, without a doubt, the spice you will use most often. Black peppercorns have a huge spectrum of quality, and the ones I recommend are Tellicherry peppercorns from India. But the most important thing is this—don't buy pepper preground in a shaker. Get a pepper mill and crack the pepper fresh, or get the little bottles that come with a little grinder top. The difference in flavor is immeasurable.

Apart from pepper I think you should have a basic spice collection to cover a lot of bases in the flavors you want to create. Spices allow us to brighten food, giving it heat, depth, and nuance. It reminds us that there is a world out there, shaped to its current state by spice routes.

The following should give you a good basic spice rack:

FENNEL SEEDS · CAYENNE · Smoked Paprika · MUSTARD POWDER

Fennel seeds	Mustard powder	Cumin seeds
Cayenne pepper	Nutmeg	Smoked paprika (aka pimentón)
Ground ginger	Cinnamon	

GROUND GINGER · NUTMEG · CINNAMON · CUMIN SEEDS

Herbs are leaves and stems of plants, and are usually green. Sometimes they are dried, like Mexican oregano, but they start out fresh. You can grow them yourself or buy them at the store.

If you buy them in those horrible little plastic caskets, you are getting ripped off. Try to buy them in larger amounts, at the farmers' market or at the Asian or Latino market. I get great deals on herbs at my local Super H Mart, the ridiculously wonderful Korean chain, where 4 ounces of thyme is $2, versus 1 ounce for $4 at the grocery store. That is a wack price difference.

Herbs provide flavor and freshness to dishes. Even a simple mincing of parsley stems can wonderfully complete a dish. Here are herbs I use a lot. I always have parsley, thyme, mint, and bay leaves on hand; the rest can be bought as you need them:

Flat-leaf parsley	Bay leaves	Tarragon
Thyme	Dill	Marjoram
Mint	Basil	Cilantro

The key to all this is tasting and smelling your spices and herbs. If you like them, use them. Of course you can follow recipes for guidance as well, but adding mint to a salad of shaved carrots and lettuce is easy. Adding chopped cilantro to a braised pork shoulder dish to serve with salsa and beans and tortillas is easy. Herbs are easy. Use more herbs.

HOW TO SEASON WITH SALT

Salt is not a spice. It is a flavor-enhancing seasoning. Our palates and taste buds are heightened by the presence of salt. It draws out moisture from food and pulls sugar to the surface. Consider a seasoned tomato: If you take a slice of raw tomato, season it with a pinch of salt, and let it sit, moisture will bead up to the cut surface. This moisture is rich in natural acids and sugars, and is magically where the flavor of the tomato is found. That extraction was made possible by the salt. That is what salt does.

I keep small ramekins with Diamond Crystal kosher salt. I like kosher salt because you can pinch it with your fingers, and over time you will learn exactly how salty one pinch of salt is for you. As I cook I add some, edging the food toward a seasoned state that makes my palate happy. I add a pinch, mix it in, and then taste. I lean on the lighter side because it is much easier to add more than remove saltiness. Diamond Crystal is my main brand because I know how it works through years of working with it. You can use Morton or a fancy sea salt, but just be consistent and get used to what the salt is doing and how much to use.

WHAT YOU NEED IN YOUR KITCHEN: POTS, PANS, UTENSILS, ETC.

Enough with the consumerist idea that you need a kitchen worthy of a magazine shoot. The reality is that I have catered for two hundred with two sternos and a large portable gas burner.

When outfitting your kitchen, the quality that you are searching for is whatever you can afford. I cooked until I was thirty years old on hand-me-down Ikea pots and a Lodge cast-iron skillet. That said, in general, pots and pans with heavy bottoms are nicer than ones that feel light and flimsy. The heavier ones even out the heat, which means they are less likely to burn your food with hot spots.

What you really need is pretty basic:

NONSTICK SKILLET (FYEO: For Your Eggs Only, or fish on occasion)

LARGE POT for stocks and pasta: 6- or 8-quart size is great

10- OR 12-INCH SKILLET OR SAUTÉ PAN (I'd call these "large")

LARGE CAST-IRON PAN

SMALL SAUCEPAN: 1- or 2-quart

LARGE SAUCEPAN: 4-quart

1 OR 2 SHEET PANS (for baking and roasting): "half-sheets," which are 18 × 13-inch or 17 × 12-inch

Assorted **MIXING BOWLS**

BLENDER (does not need to be a fancy one. I use a 30-year-old Sunbeam from a garage sale)

LITTLE BOWLS AND RAMEKINS for holding prepped ingredients

CUTTING BOARD: as big as you can afford and store

CHEF'S KNIFE

SERRATED BREAD KNIFE (this is great for anything that's hard to slice cleanly, like tomatoes)

PARING KNIFE

HONING STEEL

WHISK

HEATPROOF SILICONE SPATULA

SLOTTED SPATULA

SLOTTED SPOON

SERVING SPOONS that can double as kitchen spoons

LONG-HANDLED WOODEN SPOON, for stirring in pots

Set of **MEASURING SPOONS**

Set of **MEASURING CUPS**

Pair of **TONGS**

MEAT THERMOMETER

FRYING/CANDY THERMOMETER

VEGETABLE PEELER

COLANDER

BOX GRATER with different-sized holes

KITCHEN TOWELS: Plenty of them; they can double as oven mitts. (Except when they're wet! Never touch a hot pan with a wet towel or mitt. Steam burns. No likey.)

Things that are useful but not imperative:

FOOD PROCESSOR (a mini Cuisinart is something like $35; they are small but great.)

SIEVE

POTATO RICER OR MASHER

COOLING RACKS for sheet pans

LASAGNA PANS (can always bake in a high-sided frying pan)

DUTCH OVEN

CHEESECLOTH

KITCHEN TWINE

PASTRY BRUSH

LADLE

SPIDER/SKIMMER

SALAD SPINNER

USING A KNIFE

Think of your cutting board like a game where the goal is to keep it as clean and clear as possible. Your home base is that board, but as you progress through chores, clean well after each act, organize the product that you have prepped, and set it aside in a logical manner. What I'm saying is: Put the garlic you just chopped into a little dish, not pushed to the corner of your cutting board, so you have room to work.

Now, about that knife. A knife should be sharp, clean, and comfortable in your hand. I am right-handed, and the knife handle is in my palm, much like I would be holding a tennis racket. My thumb and the knuckle of my pointer finger are squeezing the blade to hold it steady; I'm really holding the knife there, rather than at the handle. I am not clutching it with palpable fear, rather holding it with respect. My feet are firmly on the ground, my left shoe slightly ahead of my right, about a foot and a half apart, with my hips slightly angled to the right. My left hand holds a peeled onion half down on the board, my fingers in a full claw shape, as if I am an eagle about to grab dinner from a stream. When your hand makes a claw like this, the natural lie of your fingertips is behind your knuckles, and this is on purpose: It is much better to take off a bit of your knuckle than it is to take off the end of your finger. And ideally, you don't lift the blade of your knife above those knuckles, so every precious digit is protected.

Hold the food down with your tucked-under fingertips, your thumb also behind the fingers but holding on to the bottom and side of the onion. Holding the onion there, I use the knife to slice into the onion, with a graceful, gentle push of the blade so it slides forward, through the onion. A sharp knife needs little help to do its job and is actually safer than a dull one. (You will need to push harder on a dull knife, which means it has a higher chance of slipping off the food and onto you.)

Now that you have read my exhaustive description of how to slice with a knife, just go on the Internet and look up videos on basic knife skills. It's easier if you watch them. Just make sure they're from a reputable, professional source.

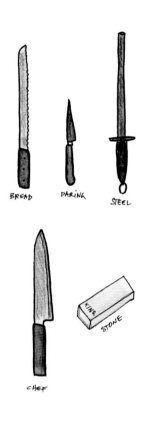

BREAD   PARING   STEEL

KING STONE

CHEF

So what kind of knife should you buy? I think the most important knife in the kitchen is a paring knife with a 4-inch blade. After that I recommend a chef's knife (choose a size that feels good in your hand; an 8-inch is great for most people) and a bread knife. Don't spend much on the bread knife because it is virtually impossible to sharpen at home so is something you will have to replace eventually.

The key to a knife is the ability to sharpen it, and that comes down to two things: a stone and a steel. A stone is meant for true sharpening and edge development and a steel is meant to just keep the edge that you have in tip-top shape. Again, I can describe the exact angles and how to push and pull your blade to sharpen or hone it or . . . you can find videos online. I'm just being honest here, folks.

CUTTING TERMS YOU SHOULD KNOW

Dice is a cube, ½ inch on each side, that will be the most common cut you will do. *Small dice* is a little smaller, *large dice* a little larger. I told you this was simple.

Brunoise is a tiny, uniform dice, ⅛ inch on each side. Doing it well is a result of doing it a lot.

Julienne is a matchstick shape, about 1½ inches long by ⅛ inch by ⅛ inch. A *baton* is a similar shape, but twice as thick.

Chop is a more rough-hewn separation of an ingredient that will be cooked or pureed to a point where the initial cut will not be apparent, like chopped tomatoes in a sauce.

Mince is a finely chopped ingredient. If *chopped* is small, *minced* is tiny.

Slice is a long even cut, and an instruction to slice will usually be accompanied by a length and thickness, such as "slice the bread so it's 6 inches long and ½ inch thick."

An *oblique* cut gives food two angled sides, supplying more surface area and reducing cooking times.

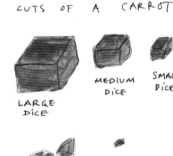

CUTS OF A CARROT

LARGE DICE

MEDIUM DICE

SMALL DICE

BRUNOISE

OBLIQUE

JULIENNE

BATONS

THE
BUILDING

BLO

THE 25 BUILDING BLOCKS

01 POACHED EGGS ......► page 24

02 VINAIGRETTE TO LIVE BY ......► page 26

03 SALAD ......► page 28

04 SAUTÉED MUSHROOMS ......► page 30

05 POTATO HASH BROWNS ......► page 32

06 BURGERS ....► page 35

07 BAKED SWEET POTATOES ......► page 38

08 FOOLPROOF RICE ......► page 40

09 BEANS (AND PEAS) ......► page 42

10 SLOW-ROASTED PORK SHOULDER ......► page 46

11 COOKING PASTA ...... ➤ page 50

12 BACK-POCKET TOMATO SAUCE ...... ➤ page 52

13 SLOW-ROASTED SOY-GARLIC TOFU ...... ➤ page 54

14 GRILLED CHEESE ...... ➤ page 56

15 SLOW-ROASTED ONIONS ...... ➤ page 58

16 ROASTED VEGETABLES ...... ➤ page 60

17 SAUTÉED GREENS ...... ➤ page 62

18 SLAW: SIMPLE AND CLASSIC ...... ➤ page 64

19 SOFRITO ...... ➤ page 66

20 ROASTED CHICKEN ...... ➤ page 68

21 COOKING STEAK [OR CHOPS OR OTHER THICK MEATS] ...... ➤ page 71

22 PAN-ROASTED FISH ...... ➤ page 74

23 POLENTA AND GRITS ...... ➤ page 76

24 PUREES: SOUPS AND BEYOND ...... ➤ page 78

25 FOUR [AND A HALF] GO-TO SUPER SIMPLE SAUCES ...... ➤ page 82

POACHED EGGS

WHY DO I WANT TO MAKE THIS?

When I was growing up it seemed like poaching eggs was the most luxurious method of egg cooking, knowledge only privy to the finest of kitchens. I had no idea it was so easy. With it you can gussy up a meal in no time at all, nesting a soft, tender poached egg into a pillow of polenta, a dressed tangle of greens, or onto a simple stew. Poached eggs can reduce cost vastly, too. Top a steak with them and you can serve smaller steaks, amped up with the power of a luscious egg, softly spilling its yolk, a picture worthy of any social media platform.

WHY DO I WANT TO LEARN TO MAKE THIS?

Poaching an egg is an exercise in controlling heat, which is one of the most important things to know in cooking. When you're boiling food, you set your heat on full blast and cook the food in roiling water. To simmer, you adjust the heat so that some bubbles come up in the pot, but not like a Jacuzzi. To poach, you're turning the heat down even more, maybe a bubble or two comes up, but really you want the water to be steaming without much activity at the surface.

The difference in these heat levels is that lower heat takes longer to cook something—duh!—but it also makes things cook more evenly. A lot of heat will cook the outside of something, maybe overcook it, before the inside is done. A gentle heat will give the insides of the food time to heat up and cook before the outsides are annihilated. A well-poached egg is silky and luxurious and, let's face it, it's a lot easier on the budget to practice with eggs than on a beautiful piece of salmon.

One more note: In eggs, you can tell the freshness by cracking them onto a plate and seeing how high the yolk sits up. The whites are thick when they're fresh and they thin out as they age. So for a full, plump poached egg, we want the freshest eggs we can find.

HOW DO I USE THIS?

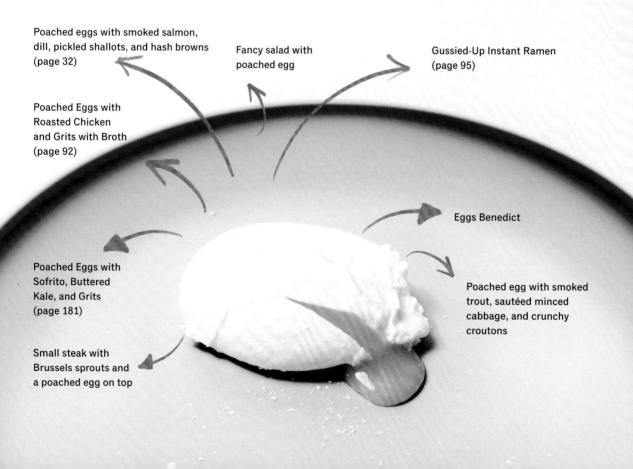

Poached eggs with smoked salmon, dill, pickled shallots, and hash browns (page 32)

Fancy salad with poached egg

Gussied-Up Instant Ramen (page 95)

Poached Eggs with Roasted Chicken and Grits with Broth (page 92)

Eggs Benedict

Poached Eggs with Sofrito, Buttered Kale, and Grits (page 181)

Poached egg with smoked trout, sautéed minced cabbage, and crunchy croutons

Small steak with Brussels sprouts and a poached egg on top

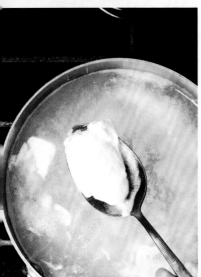

How Do I Make This?

POACHED EGGS
MAKES 2 TO 4

1 teaspoon distilled white vinegar
2 to 4 large eggs *
Kosher salt

Fill a medium or large saucepan with 2 inches of water †. Place it over medium-high heat and when it boils, add the vinegar, and reduce the heat so the water is simmering ‡. Crack each egg into an individual teacup or ramekin and have them at the ready.

With a slotted spoon, stir the water vigorously in a clockwise direction, then, one at a time, gently lower a teacup to the surface of the water and tip the egg out of the teacup §. Cook gently, never boiling, for 3 minutes for a soft yolk and just-cooked whites. Read a poem or something. Listen to *You Are My Sunshine* by Ray Charles, which is EXACTLY 3 minutes long. If you like your yolk firm, add another minute or two. Remove the eggs with the slotted spoon to a plate lined with paper towels to wick away excess moisture. Season the egg with some salt over the top and use as you wish.

---

 * If you have the time, pull the eggs out of the fridge to sit at room temperature for 15 minutes to 1 hour before you poach them. This gives them time to warm up and cook more evenly.

† To me, a "medium" saucepan is a pot that is 8 inches in diameter and at least 4 inches high. If you want to make more than 4 eggs at once, use a wider pan.

‡ Simmering means the water is very hot (about 180°F), but bubbling only gently.

§ This will help the egg white wrap over the egg to make a neat teardrop shape, and avoid loose strands of white.

WHY Do I WANT To MAKE THIS?

Vinaigrettes are infinitely flexible. They're not just salad dressings. They're sauces for a steak or piece of chicken or fish; they're great ways to add flavor to dishes. And they're infinitely adaptable flavorwise. This one is a classic—bright vinegar balanced with oil and a background of a little mustard.

A billion-dollar industry has been built on factory-made salad dressing, but with literally 1 minute and a clean mason jar, you can create your own. And the results are better than most stuff you can buy (and without stabilizers and preservatives).

WHY Do I WANT To LEARN To MAKE THIS?

Making this vinaigrette gives you a formula to create your own vinaigrettes, whether for salads or to use as a sauce for simple meat or fish—I can't stress that enough. Looking over menus and recipes I have written, vinaigrette is perhaps the most important core item I use. It finds a home everywhere as a sauce, condiment, or flavor enhancer. There are three categories of ingredients in a vinaigrette: oil, acid, and flavor. The formula is 3 parts oil to every 1 part acid (whether vinegar or lemon juice or similar), and you can flavor it however you want: Have some soy sauce from that takeout order? Some miso in the recesses of your fridge? Some finely chopped scallions or chives? The options are virtually endless.

How Do I USE THIS?

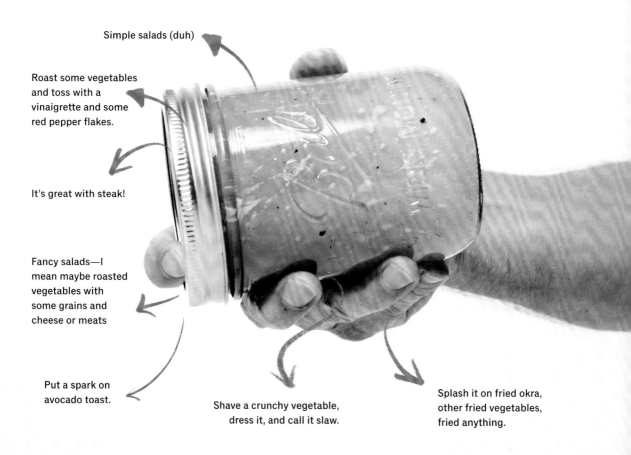

Simple salads (duh)

Roast some vegetables and toss with a vinaigrette and some red pepper flakes.

It's great with steak!

Fancy salads—I mean maybe roasted vegetables with some grains and cheese or meats

Put a spark on avocado toast.

Shave a crunchy vegetable, dress it, and call it slaw.

Splash it on fried okra, other fried vegetables, fried anything.

How Do I Make This?

CLASSIC VINAIGRETTE
MAKES ABOUT 1⅓ CUPS

1 cup extra-virgin olive oil ✱
⅓ cup cider vinegar †
1 teaspoon Dijon mustard ‡
½ teaspoon Diamond Crystal kosher
   salt, or about ¼ teaspoon Morton
   kosher salt
1 garlic clove, peeled and crushed
   with the side of a knife
Freshly ground black pepper

Place all the ingredients in a
screw-top pint jar §. Screw on
the top. Shake vigorously for
20 seconds, until combined. Done.
Shake again prior to use. This
will last on the counter easily for
a few days; in the fridge, it lasts
up to 3 weeks, even longer if you
remove the garlic before storing.
If you pull it out of the fridge, let it
come to room temp to loosen the
congealed oil, and then shake it
up well.

✱ The amount of oil you use should
be three times that of the acid. You
can tinker with this (some vinegars or
lemons are more sour than others), but
in general, 3:1 will make a vinaigrette
that is lively but not pucker-up sour.
What oil you use is up to you, but I use
a reasonably inexpensive extra-virgin
olive oil to good results.

† For basic purposes, I recommend
cider vinegar. The better your vinegar,
the better your vinaigrette. But you
can also use lemon juice, or really
anything tart and liquid.

‡ You don't have to use mustard if
you don't want. I like the flavor, but I
also use it because the mustard helps
the oil and vinegar emulsify, which
means it bonds them together and
makes the vinaigrette a bit thicker.
Without the mustard, the oil and
vinegar would separate quickly and
the vinaigrette would be pretty thin.
Not a bad thing, just up to you.

§ The jar can be a leftover pickle jar
(which does remind me that pureed
dill pickles in a vinaigrette is a thing
of beauty) or a mason jar with a clean
band and lid.

IDEAS FOR MAKING DIFFERENT VINAIGRETTES
Keep the ratio of oil to acid and adjust from there.
Nothing is off limits.

USE A DIFFERENT VINEGAR:

Sherry vinegar	Raspberry vinegar	Champagne vinegar
Rice vinegar	White wine vinegar	Balsamic vinegar

AND/OR ADD SOME:

Soy and ginger	Chopped fresh tarragon	Orange zest and curry powder
Worcestershire sauce and grainy mustard	Roasted garlic and thyme leaves	Reduced apple cider and bacon fat
Herbes de Provence	Honey and mustard	Pureed cooked scallion
Aleppo chile		

SALAD

WHY DO I WANT TO MAKE THIS?

You should love salad. People with little energy are the people who hate salad. Do not be a salad hater. And salad is easy, flexible, and fast. This one uses the core vinaigrette on page 27 to lightly dress beautiful greens. We season them with salt to maximize their flavor and then serve them showered with a great cheese. It's a far cry from that salad drowned in ranch with an odd cucumber and a lost tomato. But if that's the salad you have, you should love it still.

WHY DO I WANT TO LEARN TO MAKE THIS?

Who needs to *learn* to make a salad? It's pretty obvious, right? Yes, but . . . salads can be simple like this one, or can be composed complex meals. They can have lettuce, or be a dressed arrangement of vegetables and grains. They can have bites of roasted chicken, aged salami, or roasted tofu. They can have pickles, olives, braised vegetables, or fermented treats. If you know the basics of a great simple salad—season with salt, dress the ingredients just until they're tasty, and use a variety of textures, like crunchy and soft—you can add all kinds of stuff and come up with anything from an appetizer to a side to a full-blown meal.

Think of salad as a technique, not a recipe. Think about the possibilities with the contents of your fridge. It is a building of ingredients, lightly coated with vinaigrette and assembled. If you have heavy ingredients as part of the salad, you can build the light parts first, then dress the heavy parts and tuck them in like a Jenga stack.

HOW DO I USE THIS?

Chef's Salad (page 117)

Iceberg salad with vinaigrette, celery, Parm, and pine nuts

Spinach Salad with Pear, Pecans, Blue Cheese (page 133)

Shaved zucchini, basil, feta, pistachios

Chicken and Potato Salad with White Wine and Herbs (page 123)

Salad of roasted broccoli, goat cheese, mint

Romaine, salami, smoked mozzarella, pickled peppers, and olives

HOW DO I MAKE THIS?

CLASSIC GREEN SALAD
SERVES 4 OR MORE

1 head butter lettuce ✳

½ head romaine lettuce

1 large Belgian endive, cored and separated into leaves

1 head frisée, dark green leaves removed, cored and torn into pieces

Classic Vinaigrette (page 27)

Kosher salt and freshly ground black pepper

Finely grated Parmigiano-Reggiano cheese (to taste, but use lots)

If the lettuces are not prewashed, separate the leaves, or tear them into very big pieces, then clean † and dry them.

Place half of the greens in the largest bowl you have. Add 3 to 4 tablespoons of vinaigrette and a pinch or two of salt. Toss really well with your hands, using gentle motions. Taste it. Can you taste the salt, but not too much? Can it use more? Same with the vinaigrette. If it needs more, add some. If it's too much, add more of the greens and toss again.

Arrange the salad on a large platter. Repeat with the remaining lettuces, vinaigrette, and salt.

Season with pepper to taste and then shower with the Parmigiano all over.

✳ The butter lettuce is tender, the romaine is crunchy, and the endive and frisée have a great bitterness. I love a mix of textures, but use what you like or what you got.

† If you're washing a lot of greens, fill your (clean) sink with a few inches of cold water. Separate the leaves and agitate them in the water. Walk away for a few minutes and all the dirt will fall to the bottom. For smaller amounts, use a big bowl with a few changes of water. To dry, use a salad spinner. But NO SALAD SPINNER, NO WORRIES. Place the greens on kitchen towels. Pull all four corners together to create a bundle like you were a hobo hopping a train. Go outside. Spin your arm like you are playing air guitar. Go back inside with drier lettuces. Or just blot them dry with the towels if you don't have musical dreams.

SAUTÉED MUSHROOMS

WHY DO I WANT TO MAKE THIS?

Often when you order a side of mushrooms at a restaurant you get a limp oily mess, almost steamed to a pulp. But if you cook them well, they are golden brown, full of flavor, with a great chewy, "meaty" texture. That's what we're going for here, and you're going to love them.

WHY DO I WANT TO LEARN TO MAKE THIS?

Mushrooms are flavor bombs that can be added to almost any dish. They are full of umami, and umami is why we love soy sauce, ripe tomatoes, Parmesan, meat, and Doritos, which have flavor compounds added to them that make you wonder why you can't just eat one . . . that's umami.

This sautéing method brings out the most of those flavors. I want you to forget the names of the Kardashians, reclaim that small space in your mind, and replace it with mushroom-cooking skills. You just need to understand that mushrooms want a lot of heat and a good amount of oil or butter to sear in, and that they find companionship with garlic, thyme, and parsley. While there are lots of great, expensive mushrooms, even the thrifty white supermarket mushroom can be a wonderful treat.

HOW DO I USE THIS?

Steak with Hash Browns, Mushrooms, and Warm Vinaigrette (page 182)

Spread on toast with feta and basil.

Eat them with some lemon juice, salt, and olive oil.

Poached eggs with Salsa Verde (page 85), sautéed shiitakes, and roasted peppers

Add to a soup, sauce, or on top of a rice bowl instead of or along with meat.

Puree them into a spread for a sandwich.

Use them as a filling in an omelet.

Steamed Clams with Mushrooms, Coconut Milk, and Chiles (page 201)

Soft Polenta (page 77) with mushrooms and Grana Padano or Parmesan

How Do I Make This?

SAUTÉED MUSHROOMS
SERVES 2 AS A SIDE DISH

¾ pound shiitake mushrooms, stems discarded *

1 teaspoon Diamond Crystal kosher salt, or ½ teaspoon Morton kosher salt

3 tablespoons canola oil

1 tablespoon unsalted butter

2 to 4 sprigs fresh thyme

Cut the mushrooms into bite-size pieces; usually quartering them does the trick. Toss the mushrooms with the salt in a bowl. Transfer the mushrooms to a sieve set over a bowl and let sit for 20 minutes †. Then spread the shiitakes out on a paper towel and press and blot them with more paper towel to absorb moisture.

In a very large sauté pan, heat the canola oil and butter over medium-high heat. Once the butter is done foaming, stir the shiitakes into the pan to coat them, then spread them out. Leave the shiitakes alone and allow them to get a nice brown color on them, about 6 minutes.

Stir in the thyme sprigs. Cook for another 3 minutes ‡. Once you've achieved a good color on the shiitakes, transfer them to a platter lined with paper towels to absorb excess oil. Serve warm.

---

* Shiitakes are commonly available, have a beautiful flavor, and have a firmness that holds up in cooking. One drawback is that you have to tear their stems off, which are too tough for eating. (They're great thrown into a stock or soup for flavor, however.) If you're not using shiitakes, most other mushroom stems are fine for eating; just cut them up along with the rest of the mushroom. If there's visible dirt, rub it off with a paper towel.

† You salt the mushrooms in advance to pull the moisture out, since less water = less steam = more caramelization.

‡ Shiitakes tend to cook quickly. If you're using other kinds of mushrooms and cut into thicker chunks, you may need to cook them longer. No big deal. Just keep an eye on their color—you want them nicely browned.

POTATO HASH BROWNS

How Do I Make This?

HASH BROWNS
MAKES 4 HASH BROWNS

1 medium sweet onion ✳
1 pound russet potatoes †
1½ teaspoons Diamond Crystal
kosher salt, or 1 teaspoon Morton
kosher salt
¼ teaspoon freshly ground black
pepper
3 tablespoons oil (or, even better,
Clarified Butter, recipe follows)

Finely chop the onion and place it in a large bowl.

Peel the potatoes. Using a grater or a food processor, grate the peeled potatoes, working quickly to avoid oxidation ‡. Place the grated potatoes in a clean kitchen towel and wring out the excess liquid over the sink. Squeeze hard! Mix the potatoes with the onions, salt, and pepper.

Heat a large skillet over medium-high heat. Add the oil (or clarified butter) and when it just wisps a little smoke, add the potatoes carefully to the pan, in 4 equal piles. Gently press down and form the potatoes into 4-inch

rounds, about 1 inch high §. After 3 to 5 minutes, they should turn golden brown on the bottom and around the edges. Adjust the temperature to keep them cooking but not getting too dark.

Once they're browned, gently flip the hash browns with a slotted spatula. Continue cooking until the other side is golden brown, another 3 to 5 minutes.

Remove the hash browns to a plate lined with paper towels, or even better, to a cooling rack set over a sheet pan, to rest and cool slightly.

✱ This can be a Vidalia, a Maui, or just a white onion. "Sweet" onions are so named because they don't have as much of that burning punch other onions can have.

† Russet (aka Idaho) potatoes are key. Their higher starch content means crispy results. Avoid types like Yukon Gold or red potatoes. These creamier types have their wonderful place in cooking, but this is not their arena.

‡ You know how potatoes turn gray-brown after you cut them and let them hang out for a while? That's oxidation.

§ They will settle down to about ½ inch high by the time they are done. Don't pack them too hard, though, as you want the butter to bubble up through gaps of the potatoes.

CLARIFIED BUTTER
MAKES ABOUT 1½ CUPS

Butter is composed of fat, water, and milk solids; clarifying it is the process of removing the water and milk solids so the fat can get hotter for cooking without burning. It is easy as pie to do.

1 pound unsalted butter, cubed

Place the butter in a saucepan over medium-high heat. It will boil and foam. Reduce the heat to a gentle bubble and continue cooking to vaporize the water in the butter. The milk solids will begin to brown lightly and sink to the bottom. When this happens, turn off the heat and let it rest slightly. Strain through a coffee filter into a clean jar, discarding the milk solids that end up in the filter. You can keep this in the fridge or on the counter.

WHY Do I WANT To MAKE THIS?

You want to make this because hash browns like this are DELICIOUS. Hash browns are pan-fried loosely formed grated or shredded potatoes, and I add a little onion for flavor. I like food that is constantly crave worthy, and hash browns hit that note harder than Animal on the drum set.

I have longed to open my own version of a Waffle House, the ubiquitous Southern chain of fast-served food. I would cook the same food, wear a paper hat, but just use good ingredients and technique. That's why *I* want to make hash browns, I guess, but even if you don't want to open a Waffle House, you're going to love these anyway.

WHY Do I WANT To LEARN To MAKE THIS?

Everyone loves potatoes in many forms, but learning to make hash browns gives you something special with little effort, and they're great on their own or as a foundation to a dish—top 'em to make a meal. And they're a lot less messy than making French fries.

HOW Do I USE THIS?

Obviously the first thing that comes to mind is a perfect hash brown on your breakfast plate, but they can be used in so many ways to make a meal. Top them with all kinds of stuff or serve them on the side.

Serve with fried eggs, Salsa Rossa (page 84), and bacon.

Serve with a Poached Egg (page 25), Roasted Broccoli (page 61), and Slow-Roasted Soy-Garlic Tofu (page 55).

Top with smoked salmon and dill sour cream.

Hash Browns with Goat Cheese and Roasted Red Peppers (page 170)

Hash browns scattered, smothered, covered, and stuffed (go to a Waffle House at least once)

Serve with a salad and a chunk of cheese for lunch.

Top with hummus, pickled chiles, sesame, and chives.

WHY Do I WANT To MAKE THiS?

Because burgers are good. And good burgers are great.

WHY Do I WANT To LEARN To MAKE THiS?

Come on. Everyone should know how to cook a burger. (Vegetarians may be excused.) But a burger is more than a burger. I want you to think of it more as a quality-driven chopped steak. You can put it on a bun, or use it in any application in which you would want a luscious serving of protein.

How Do I USE THiS OR MAKE THiS DIFFERENT?

Finely chop some mushrooms in a food processor and add them to the meat as you blend the burger mixture.

Use ground lamb or pork instead (or chicken or turkey, but cook those all the way through).

Use a different cheese that you wouldn't think about. Cream cheese is ridiculously good on a burger.

Add spices if you want.

Lose the bun and have a gluten-free experience.

Make a Luxe Patty Melt (page 128).

Make it a base for some bean salad.

Top it with kimchi and pickled radishes.

How Do I Make This?

BURGERS
MAKES 4 BURGERS

1½ pounds cold ground beef (80% lean/20% fat) ✳

1 tablespoon Diamond Crystal kosher salt, or 2 teaspoons Morton kosher salt

Freshly ground black pepper

1 teaspoon canola oil

4 slices American cheese

4 sesame seed buns

4 slices large red tomato, if in season

2 dill pickles, thinly sliced

½ medium yellow onion, sliced into thin rounds

4 leaves butter lettuce

Mustard and ketchup, for serving

Combine the cold beef and three-quarters of the salt in a medium bowl. Mix well, by hand, until the salt is integrated and the texture of the beef is a little smoother than it was †. Divide the meat into 4 portions and gently roll them into balls. Place the meatballs, one at a time, between greased pieces of wax paper and press down with a heavy pan‡ to make patties about ½ inch thick. Smooth out the edges and your patties will be ready for action.

Heat a 10- to 12-inch cast-iron skillet§ over medium-high heat. Season the burgers, on both sides, with the remaining salt and pepper to taste. When the pan is hot, add the oil, and when the oil is shimmering-hot, nearly smoking, lay in the burgers. Probably you can get 2 patties in at a time;

don't crowd the pan. Cook until well browned, about 3 minutes, then flip them over. Cook for 1½ minutes on the other side. This should get you to medium; if you like it more or less cooked, just adjust the cooking time.

Remove the burgers to a plate and immediately top each with a slice of cheese. Let the burgers rest for a few minutes. Resting lets all of the juice that has run to the center of the meat return to where it came from.

Place a burger on the bottom of each bun, and then tomato, pickles, onion, and lettuce. Place the burger tops on each and serve with mustard and ketchup.

Wipe out the pan and repeat with the remaining patties.

✳ Look for really fresh ground beef, avoiding graying beef, a sign of age. Ground beef is often labeled with percentages of lean and fat; the one you want is 80% lean and 20% fat. The fat will help keep the burger moist.

† Some people like a really loose, tender burger and advise you to just barely handle the beef. But I like to knead the cold beef a little with my (clean) hands to develop the protein texture that will hold it together when you patty it up. The salt will season the beef all the way through, and not just be a scant smattering on the outside of the patty.

‡ I like to smoosh the patties down because it creates flat surfaces, which contact the hot skillet and get nicely browned.

§ Cast-iron is great because it retains heat for a good, browning sear. Get that pan really hot. Open the window and turn on whatever hood vent you have, if you have one. No apartment I lived in, from age seventeen to twenty-four, had a hood vent, so the broom was usually used as a long poker to turn off the smoke detector.

BAKED SWEET POTATOES

WHY Do I Want To Make This?

If your only experience with sweet potatoes is with marshmallows and maple syrup—dessert pretending to be a side dish—having it more simply shows off how well it balances sweet and savory. Sweet potatoes are delicious and take savory flavors well, and they're inexpensive and super nutritious. They feed much of the world with their vast variety of uses. Clean it. Fork it. Bake it.

WHY Do I Want To Learn To Make This?

The technique here can pretty much be applied to any dense vegetable you crave: regular potatoes, large carrots, rutabaga, celery root, and winter squash. Once a sweet potato is cooked, you can cut it open, nice and hot, and eat it. Or you can puree it for whipped sweet potatoes. Or take it out of the fridge, dice it up, and hash it. Use it as a vegetable or a starch, or as the base of a meal with different accompaniments. But it can all start with a simple bake.

How Do I Use This?

If it's well-cooked and soft throughout, you can scoop out the flesh, throw it in a food processor or use a potato masher, mash in butter and salt and pepper to taste and have whipped sweet potatoes. Add some chile flakes and maple syrup, too, and you'll be talking about it for days. Or blend some hot chicken stock into *that* and you can have a creamy sweet potato soup.

If it's a little less cooked, dice it up and sauté it with greens and olive oil, or leftover corned beef and cabbage, for a great hash.

Put diced sweet potatoes in tortillas with some spicy salsa, Cotija cheese, and cilantro for tacos.

Or sauté them in a little oil with tofu and scallions, and dress it with a vinaigrette (see page 27) flavored with soy sauce.

Sweet Potato Hash with Salsa Rossa and Sour Cream (page 177)

Sweet Potato and Spicy Green Tomato Shakshuka (page 158)

How Do I Make This?

BAKED SWEET POTATOES
SERVES 2 TO 4

2 medium sweet potatoes
(about 8 ounces each)

1 tablespoon unsalted butter,
at room temperature,
plus more for serving

1 teaspoon Diamond Crystal
kosher salt, or ½ teaspoon Morton
kosher salt

Preheat the oven to 400°F＊. Line
a sheet pan with a silicone mat or
foil or top it with a wire rack.†

Wash the sweet potatoes under
running water to get any dirt
off, then dry them with a kitchen
towel. Rub each sweet potato all
over with ½ tablespoon butter.
Sprinkle them evenly with the
salt‡ and place on the prepared
sheet pan. Transfer to the oven
and bake for 45 minutes to
1 hour§.

Cut them in half, slather with
some butter, maybe season with
more salt, and eat. Or cool them
to use in numerous dishes later
on. They will keep for 4 days in
the fridge, wrapped tightly in
plastic wrap.

＊ Setting your oven to 400°F will
cook the sweet potatoes evenly and
relatively quickly. A good all-around
cooking (or reheating) temp is
350°F. Anything higher than 425°F is
considered a hot oven.

† A wire rack set into a sheet pan
is a great way of letting your sweet
potatoes cook evenly all around (they
won't be sitting on the hot metal,
which would cook that side more than
the others). But if you don't have a
rack, no big deal; just set the potatoes
on a silicone mat or sheet of foil on the
sheet pan . . . this will make cleanup a
lot easier.

‡ You are seasoning the potato ahead
of cooking to get some of that salt to
cook into it. Sweet potatoes definitely
need salt to bring out their flavor.

§ After about 30 minutes, I will begin
checking the doneness by poking the
sweet potatoes with a sharp knife. If
you can get the knife in pretty easily
but with a little effort, it'll be firm
enough to dice up later and use for
hash or other uses. If the potato is so
soft the knife goes in with no effort,
then it'll be good for mashing or
pureeing. If you just wanna eat it, the
doneness is up to your taste.

FOOLPROOF RICE

WHY Do I WANT To MAKE THIS?

I guess I don't *really* need to explain to you why rice is a good food. Rice is a daily staple of most of the world, so if you learn how to make rice, it means you get a GLOBAL CITIZEN BADGE. OK, it's also a versatile base for a meal. You can make a bunch at once, eat what you want, and have a flexible leftover that can be transformed into many dishes.

WHY Do I WANT To LEARN To MAKE THIS?

The method of cooking rice below is different than you may be used to, but it means you get good results each time. No more measuring, no more hoping it doesn't come out gummy or hard in the middle. Let's take the guesswork out of fluffy rice. The easiest way to cook rice well is to think of it as a pasta. And you can use this method for all kinds of grains, like quinoa, farro, etc.

HOW Do I USE THIS?

Roast a chicken, or cook a steak, put some rice next to it, and let it sop up the juices.

Reheat the rice in chicken or vegetable stock, with bites of tofu or meat or chicken, a squeeze of lemon, a touch of soy sauce, and maybe some herbs for a warming stew.

Toast some curry powder in butter and toss it with hot rice with cashews, yogurt, and a squeeze of lime.

Top it with cooked beans (see page 44) and their broth, or sauté it with the beans to make a pilaf.

Rice is a great companion to really anything, especially anything stewy or saucy or juicy.

Fried rice! It's an excellent way to turn bits and pieces of leftovers into a great meal (see Fried Rice with Pork and Kimchi, page 114).

Rice is life. Make some rice.

HOW DO I MAKE THIS?

FOOLPROOF RICE
**MAKES ABOUT 2¹/₂ CUPS
(SERVES 2)** ✳

1 cup basmati or other long-grain rice †

8 fresh bay leaves (optional)

2 tablespoons Diamond Crystal kosher salt, or 4 teaspoons Morton kosher salt

1 tablespoon unsalted butter, cubed

Put the rice in a big bowl and swish it around in cold water. Pour the water out and repeat a couple times until the water is noticeably clearer ‡. If you keep dropping rice into the sink, you can pour the rice into a sieve, dump it back in the bowl, and repeat.

In a large pot, combine 4 quarts water, the bay leaves (if using— they taste good), and salt. Bring to a boil over high heat, then stir in the rice, and start timing. Stir the rice often as it cooks to keep the kernels from sticking. At 10 minutes, take a few grains out with a slotted spoon and taste them. The rice should have just a *touch* of firmness; it'll finish cooking as it sits to drain.

Carefully drain the rice in a fine-mesh sieve. Allow to drain for 2 minutes, carefully stirring the rice a bit to help the water and steam get out. Toss the rice with butter in a large bowl until all the rice is coated evenly.

Remove the bay leaves and serve. Or, to save the rice for later, spread it out on a large platter or sheet pan, so it cools quickly. When it's room temp, pack it up and put it in the fridge, where it will keep for 4 to 5 days pretty easily. Reheat it in the microwave, or by sautéing it in a touch of oil or butter in a hot pan.

✳ 1 cup raw rice makes enough to serve 2 people, depending on how hungry they are. You can make more rice easily with this method. Just add more rice (and butter, if using). I'd go up to 4 cups of raw rice at once.

† In general, there are three categories of rice: short-, medium-, and long-grain. For this core technique I want to concentrate on long-grain, which generally cooks up the fluffiest. Examples of commonly available long-grain rice are jasmine, basmati, and Carolina Gold, amongst many others. (Don't use parboiled rice for this.) I like basmati a lot. It is widely available and naturally nutty-flavored, and the key rice for Indian cuisines.

‡ You rinse rice to wash off the powdery starch that coats the kernels, which can turn gummy and gluey if left on.

BEANS (AND PEAS)

WHY Do I WANT To MAKE THIS?

If you are tired of instant ramen, or if you like foods that make their own sauce, or if you just like food, then dried beans are your friend. They are cheap. They plump up to three times their size, and have a ton of protein, fiber, and vitamins. Beans power you through the day, and yes you can make jokes about that. I love beans so much I couldn't settle on just one basic bean recipe, so turn the page for two: black beans with bacon, and chickpeas cooked with some sweet vegetables.

Dried beans are a far cry from the world of food that is all about colorful packaging and ultraconvenience. But they are easy to make, honestly delicious, and super versatile—creamy, rich, and meaty-tasting just by themselves. You can eat them with their cooking liquid—which is naturally tasty—or strain them out and toss them with rice or vegetables. You can eat them as a great side instead of potatoes or rice with meat or fish, dress them like a salad, and use the broth instead of chicken or vegetable stock. Or you can puree them and make dips like hummus in a flash. And all you had to do was soak and boil them for a while. Even the very best beans are just a few dollars a pound, and standard ones—which are also good—just a few cents.

And while I love cooking beans and peas from dried, there's nothing wrong with canned beans for a quick dish. Drain, rinse, and use them any of the ways at right that don't require the bean broth. Or just use chicken or vegetable broth to replace the liquid.

WHY Do I WANT To LEARN To MAKE THIS?

There are two recipes here—one for black beans and one for chickpeas. And while they have different flavorings, the basic method is the same, and can work for pretty much any dried bean or pea. There are tons of varieties, such as navy, kidney, borlotti, lima, black-eyed peas, and favas, and they all have different flavors and textures. A bag can go a long way—1 pound of dried beans can feed 8 people. Learn this technique and you will find yourself in a very bean-ificial position.

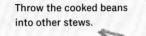

HOW DO I USE THIS?

Throw the cooked beans into other stews.

Serve with rice, for a combination as old as time.

Stir some Red Sofrito (page 67) into a bowl of beans along with some broth and serve with sour cream, chives, and cilantro on top.

Add chunks of sausage or other meat to the beans and broth and eat them like a stew.

Mix with rice, vinaigrette (see page 27), and small cuts of vegetables and herbs.

Stuff the beans in a quesadilla.

Use the bean broth in place of stock for other soups or stews.

Add the beans to salads for a protein punch.

Puree the beans in a blender with their broth, along with Slow-Roasted Onions (page 59) and celery, to make a rich soup. Maybe top it with some Salsa Verde (page 85) or Cucumber Raita (page 86).

Drain the beans (keeping the bean broth) and puree the beans with tahini, lemon juice, olive oil, salt, and a little garlic for a hummus. If too thick, splash in a little bean broth.

Sauté drained cooked beans with butter, small-diced vegetables, and a squeeze of lemon for a great side.

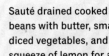

How Do I Make This?

What follows are two recipes, for very different beans (or peas) with different flavors, textures, and results. But they're also proof that the method for them is basically the same, and you can swap in pretty much any dried bean or pea (except lentils—you don't need to soak lentils and they cook really fast, like 20 to 30 minutes usually) and use whatever flavor ingredients (I call them "bean kits") you like.

BACONY BLACK BEANS
MAKES ABOUT 8 CUPS
(SERVES 4 TO 6)

1 cup dried black beans

1 tablespoon Diamond Crystal kosher salt, or 2 teaspoons Morton kosher salt, and some more to finish

FOR THE BEAN KIT

1 large yellow onion, peeled and halved

1 medium carrot, peeled and cut into 1-inch lengths

2 celery stalks, cut into 2-inch lengths

2 garlic cloves, peeled and crushed with the side of a knife

2 ounces bacon, uncut or slices

2 bay leaves

CHICKPEAS
MAKES ABOUT 8 CUPS
(SERVES 4 TO 6)

1 cup dried chickpeas

1 tablespoon Diamond Crystal kosher salt, or 2 teaspoons Morton kosher salt, and some more to finish

FOR THE BEAN KIT

1 yellow onion, peeled and halved

1 medium carrot, peeled and cut into 1-inch lengths

2 celery stalks, cut into 2-inch lengths

2 garlic cloves, peeled and crushed with the side of a knife

2 bay leaves

½ teaspoon coarsely ground black pepper

Spread the dried beans/chickpeas on a sheet pan. Sort through them and pick out any tiny rocks ✳ or things that look just not right. Place in a colander and rinse the beans under cold water, drain, and then put them in a container and fill it with cold water to come 2 inches above the beans. Mix in 1 tablespoon of salt. Refrigerate and let soak for at least 8 and up to 12 hours †.

Drain the beans/chickpeas again, pour them into a big pot, and cover with cold water by 2 inches. Add the bean kit.

Bring the water to a boil over high heat. When the water reaches a boil, reduce the heat to a simmer. Stir every 5 minutes or so, if you remember, so the beans cook evenly. Once the beans are tender ‡, add salt to taste, cover, and remove from the heat. Ideally let them sit for 30 minutes to plump up in the liquid, or eat them right away if you can't wait. Discard the onion, carrot, celery, and bay leaves. Transfer leftovers to a container to store in the fridge, for 5 days or so.

✳ You won't find rocks often, but sometimes they're hiding in there.

† The soaking slowly starts the process of rehydrating the beans. The beans will absorb water, like a pampering bath, plumping and reducing the time you need to cook them. It helps them cook more evenly, too. They will be plumper after a 12-hour soak than with an 8-hour soak, of course. If you didn't plan ahead, you can still cook them without soaking; just know you'll have to cook them a bit longer.

‡ There is no real way to predict how long it will take beans to cook; it depends on the variety, their age, and the batch. Sometimes it's 45 minutes after soaking, sometimes it's 2 hours. Plan on 1 hour to 1 hour 30 minutes. Start tasting them at 45 minutes; if they're still hard, let them keep going, and check every 10 or 15 minutes. And if they're cooking for a long time, the water level might get too low; just add more water to keep them covered.

SLOW-ROASTED PORK SHOULDER
(YES, YOU CAN DO THIS)

WHY DO I WANT TO MAKE THIS?

Imagine a massive roast of beautifully cooked pork, browned all over and glistening. The meat is so luscious you can pull it into soft bites without a knife. This is absolutely, completely within your grasp. Trust me. The cut of pork is inexpensive and it's a very simple process that produces a centerpiece, or that can be torn to use in lettuce wraps with pickles and honey mustard, or crisped in a pan with a touch of bacon fat to be used as a carnitas-esque filling for tacos or burritos.

And you can impress 8 of your best friends, or 4 to 6 and have enough left to feed you for days. It takes a while, yes, but is also something that should be in your arsenal.

WHY DO I WANT TO LEARN TO MAKE THIS?

This is a classic slow-roast/braise technique for a large cut of sinewy meat, i.e., a cheaper cut. Pork shoulder (or lamb shoulder, or beef shoulder roasts, which this technique also works for) is much more inexpensive than the "prime" cuts like rib roasts or loins. Shoulders are thought to be tougher meats, but if you treat them right, they are delicious and tender. This is one beautiful, simple way to treat a shoulder right.

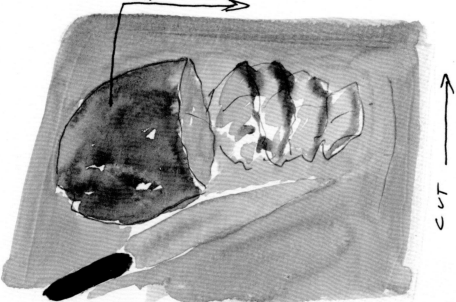

How Do I Use This?

This is either a super impressive centerpiece to your table for a party, or a super flexible all-purpose meat for filling tacos, sandwiches, and more.

Shred the meat and crisp it in some oil or, even better, bacon fat, for carnitas tacos, along with salsa, diced onions, and cilantro.

Tear and crisp it with some cooked chickpeas (see page 44) and serve with pita and Cucumber Raita (page 86).

Serve with Salsa Verde (page 85) and Soft Polenta (page 77).

Cuban Grilled Cheese (page 125)

Lettuce wraps with rice and hot sauce, honey mustard, or anything that will give it a kick

Pork hash

How Do I Make This?

SLOW-ROASTED PORK SHOULDER
SERVES 8 TO 10
(OR A SMALLER GROUP WITH
PLENTY OF LEFTOVERS)

6-pound bone-in, skinless pork
  shoulder (butt) ✳

2 tablespoons Diamond Crystal
  kosher salt, or 4 teaspoons Morton
  kosher salt

1 tablespoon light brown sugar

1 tablespoon Spanish smoked
  paprika †

½ teaspoon crushed red pepper
  flakes

1 tablespoon canola oil

2 cups chicken stock

1 medium onion, quartered

1 cup orange juice

Rinse the pork shoulder under cold water. Pat it dry with paper towels and then set it on a large baking pan, something with sides ‡, like a lasagna pan. In a small bowl, mix together the salt, brown sugar, smoked paprika, and pepper flakes. Evenly sprinkle the spice mixture all over the pork, turning it over to hit all of it. Place it fat-side up on the baking pan, cover it with plastic wrap, and refrigerate for 8 to 12 hours §.

Arrange an oven rack in the lowest position and preheat the oven to 275°F.

Set a heavy ovenproof pot, like a Dutch oven or soup pot, large enough to fit the pork in, over medium-high heat. Add the oil and when the oil is shimmering-hot, add the pork, fat-side down. Sear the pork for 5 to 10 minutes, until nicely browned, and then carefully turn it over. Add the chicken stock, onion, and orange juice. Cover the pot and transfer to the oven.

Cook until the meat is tender enough to be pierced with a fork with little resistance, 5 to 6 hours. Remove it from the oven ¶ and let it sit, covered, for 30 minutes, to rest #.

Carve or shred it up as you wish—just make sure to cut against the grain if you are carving.

✳ In spite of its name, a pork butt (or Boston butt) is not a butt at all, but the upper shoulder cut of pork. (The lower is a ham.) Because the shoulder works a lot, it has a lot of flavor, and tendons and sinew to support the role it plays, which soften and melt in low, slow cooking like this. (Bone-in meat tastes better, too.) It is vastly different from something like a tenderloin, a muscle that doesn't really do much, resulting in tenderness with short cooking times. This technique also works for other large, sinewy cuts like lamb or beef shoulder roasts. The cooking time will change depending on the size and weight of the meat; ask your butcher for advice.

† Also called pimentón, this is great stuff. It adds a wonderful smoky flavor to anything.

‡ You want it to be able to hold the juices that will come out of the pork.

§ This 8- to 12-hour salting is called "dry brining." It helps the salt work itself into the meat and season it inside. It also helps tenderize it. This process works with all kinds of meat (but not fish), if you have time.

¶ Protect your hand with DRY kitchen towels or mitts! Never wet or damp towels! They will steam if you touch hot pans with them, and steam burns.

After any meat cookery, a good long rest time helps the juices settle back into the meat.

COOKING PASTA

WHY DO I WANT TO MAKE THIS?

Um, because everyone loves spaghetti?

WHY DO I WANT TO LEARN TO MAKE THIS?

There is a lot of mythology about how to cook pasta. No, you don't throw it against the wall to see if it's done. No, you don't add oil to the cooking water.

Al dente is a term thrown out a lot. It translates as "to the tooth," meaning the pasta should have a slight firmness to it when done, not be mushy throughout. That said, if you bite into pasta and see a layer of dry white, this is not al dente, it is just undercooked.

Just follow these steps and your pasta will be perfectly cooked every time. The key is copious amounts of boiling water, with a salt level just short of the ocean, to season the pasta on the inside.

HOW DO I USE THIS?

Of course, pasta with tomato sauce is a classic. And you can riff on that any number of ways—add some sausage, or eggplant, or cubes of mozzarella along with some Parmesan. But pasta itself is a great foundation for sautés of vegetables or meats with olive oil and garlic; you don't have to always think of making a separate "sauce." Just cook pasta well, maybe add butter and Parmesan, have that other stuff also cooked in a pan, maybe use a little bit of the pasta cooking water to moisten it all, and: dinner.

How Do I Make This?

PASTA
SERVES 4 AS A MAIN COURSE, 6 TO 8 AS A STARTER

1 pound pasta* (spaghetti, penne, whatever)

Kosher salt

Fill a large pot with 4 quarts water and set it over high heat. When it's hot, add plenty of salt†.

Bring the water to a rolling boil and carefully add the pasta. (If it's spaghetti, don't break the strands, they will soften and fit in the pot.) Stir for the first minute or so‡. Keep the lid off§.

Look at your pasta package for a guide to the cooking time¶. The pasta is done when it has a cooked consistency, with still a touch of resistance to the tooth. Scoop out the pasta with a long-handled sieve, a skimmer, or tongs. You could also ladle out and save a cup of the pasta cooking water# and then drain the pasta in a colander. Sauce it right away.

* This recipe is for dried pasta. If you want to use fresh pasta, 1 pound will feed more like 3 people than 4, and it will cook much faster than dried, like just a couple of minutes.

† Give it a taste. It should be saline but not as much as sea water. It should taste pleasantly salty. It may be saltier than you are used to for pasta water, but that's why you are here learning the right way. The salted water seasons the pasta from within as it cooks.

‡ Stirring the pasta right when it gets into the boiling water is the key to not having the pasta stick together.

§ Covering the pot will cause the water to boil over, and be a hot mess on your stove.

¶ The pasta box has no idea at what altitude you live, what size your pot is, etc. Use your senses. Cooking is always dynamic. Taste a piece a minute or two *before* the suggested cooking time. If it's still hard in the middle, or if you see white when you bite into it, keep cooking, and checking again every minute or so.

The water you saved is good for moistening (or stretching) the sauce if need be.

BACK-POCKET TOMATO SAUCE

WHY DO I WANT TO MAKE THIS?

You need a core tomato sauce to get through life. Yes, premade jarred tomato sauce is one of the easiest things to buy. But it tastes better and fresher if you make it at home, and it's also one of the easiest things you can make. You want to feel that satisfaction.

WHY DO I WANT TO LEARN TO MAKE THIS?

The recipe here takes just five ingredients—tomatoes, olive oil, garlic, basil, and salt—and makes them sing in harmony. But the technique of first toasting the garlic in the olive oil before adding the tomatoes gives the garlic a warm, sweet flavor that permeates the sauce. It's totally different than if you just threw everything in the pot and turned on the heat; it creates layers of flavor.

HOW DO I USE THIS?

Toss some cooked ziti or penne in it, stir in some chunks of mozzarella or spoonfuls of ricotta and some chopped roasted vegetables. Pour pasta into a baking dish, top with some more mozz, and bake it at 400°F until browned and bubbling.

Add it to cooked chickpeas (see page 44) with some scallion and some minced jalapeño, then garnish with sour cream and toasted cumin.

Add capers to it for some salty pop. Serve it under Pan-Roasted Salmon (page 75) with a squeeze of lemon.

Add some cream, stock, and dry vermouth and puree to a smooth texture. Voilà: tomato bisque, just like in a fancy restaurant.

Sear some stew meat or sausages until browned, smother it in tomato sauce, and gently simmer it until the meat is tender and delicious.

Make meatballs and simmer them in the sauce (see Spaghetti and Meatballs, page 96).

Toss with pasta and Parm and basil, of course.

Bake chicken or fish right in it.

Use it as a pizza sauce.

You can feed a civilization on a simple marinara.

Add ancho chile powder and use it as an enchilada sauce.

HOW DO I MAKE THIS?

BACK-POCKET TOMATO SAUCE
MAKES ABOUT 1½ QUARTS

½ cup extra-virgin olive oil

8 garlic cloves

2 (28-ounce) cans whole peeled
tomatoes ✱

4 sprigs fresh basil

1 teaspoon Diamond Crystal kosher
salt, or ½ teaspoon Morton kosher
salt, plus more to taste

In a large pot, heat the olive oil
over low heat. Thinly slice the
garlic † and add it to the oil.

In a large bowl, crush the tomatoes
with your hands. When the garlic
is golden, add the tomatoes
with their juices, the basil, and
the salt. Stir, increase the heat
to medium-high, and bring to
a simmer. Reduce the heat to
a lazy bubble ‡ and cook for
45 minutes, stirring occasionally.
Taste the sauce. You're looking
for a deep, rich flavor. Season it
with salt §. Remove from the heat,
discard the basil, and ladle the
sauce into clean containers. Cool
on the counter for 30 minutes and
then store in the fridge for up to
1 week, or freeze for a few months.

✱ I love canned whole San Marzano
tomatoes from Italy. They come from
a consortium of tomato farmers who
grow the best tomatoes for canning
in the entire world. You can substitute
fresh tomatoes, but they just require a
little more work to stem and chop and
do not possess the consistency that
the canned ones provide. However,
you can wing it and make delicious
sauce as long as you taste as you go
and keep cooking and adjusting the
salt until it tastes good.

† Slice the garlic as thinly as Paulie
does it in the movie *Goodfellas*. Are
you old enough to remember that
movie? Regardless, it is a great food
moment in an amazing movie.

‡ You are trying to encourage flavor
with heat, not desiccate the sauce,
so keep the heat pretty low. The more
a sauce cooks, the more water is
evaporated from it and concentrates
it. But it also changes the flavor, from
a bright, fresh flavor to a deeper,
mellower, "cooked" one. So a low-
temperature cook helps you balance
those two.

§ If the sauce feels like it's missing
"something," it's probably salt, unless
it already tastes "salty." Stir in a pinch
and taste it. Do it again. And again,
until the flavor feels fuller and more
delicious, but not salty.

SLOW-ROASTED SOY-GARLIC TOFU

WHY DO I WANT TO MAKE THIS?

Tofu is not just for vegetarians. It can taste great and is super duper cheap for the protein it packs. If your introduction to tofu is bland cubes pretending to be meat, prepare to be amazed: tofu steeped in soy sauce and garlic, roasted until firm and caramelized, is an entirely different animal. Only it's not made from animals.

Once you make it, it's great in sandwiches, as a quick protein you can drop into stews or soups, or easily dressed as a protein addition to a bowl with rice or grains and vegetables.

WHY DO I WANT TO LEARN TO MAKE THIS?

I love tofu in its many forms, from custard-soft to dense, meat-like slices. For people who aren't super familiar with it, though, it can seem bland. This technique will help pull flavor into the tofu. The key is to lightly salt and then press the tofu, to squeeze out any extra water. Then a nice, long marinade that will season the tofu.

HOW ELSE CAN I MARINATE IT?

This marinade imparts great flavor, but leaves the tofu pretty flexible in terms of what it can be served with. Feel free to add, subtract, mix, and match ingredients and sauces you like to create your own flavor of marinade for the tofu. Smoked paprika and garlic, lemon zest and thyme, miso and lime, sesame oil and ginger, minced olives and mustard . . . those are only a few options that you could play with. Basically, if something tastes good to you, it will taste good in a tofu marinade.

HOW DO I USE THIS?

Toss roasted tofu into sautéed greens with minced fresh ginger.

Serve roasted tofu over leftover rice and beans with some cucumber and sesame seeds.

Stew some roasted tofu with tomatoes, oregano, garlic, and cumin.

Stew some beans with stock and finish it with cubes of roasted tofu.

Make some tacos with the tofu, Sautéed Mushrooms (page 31), salsa, chopped onion, and cilantro.

Sauté some ground pork, chopped roasted tofu, minced ginger, garlic, and chiles, dressed with oyster sauce and soy sauce for lettuce wraps.

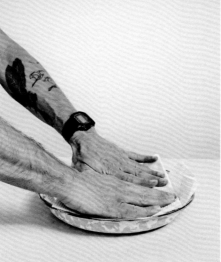

How Do I Make This?

SLOW-ROASTED
SOY-GARLIC TOFU
SERVES 2 TO 4

1 (14-ounce) package firm
  or extra-firm tofu ✱

Kosher salt

2 tablespoons extra-virgin olive oil

2 tablespoons reduced-sodium
  soy sauce

1 garlic clove, minced

1 tablespoon sherry vinegar

Pat the tofu dry with a paper towel. Ideally, line a colander with cheesecloth, clean dish cloth, or a coffee filter. Lightly, and I mean lightly, sprinkle salt on the tofu. Place the tofu in the lined colander and place another piece of lining over the tofu. Then place something of moderate weight on top of the tofu and let it sit 30 minutes to 1 hour to press out excess water †. Slice the pressed tofu into 6 rectangles ¾ inch thick. (You can achieve similar results by simply slicing the tofu out of the package and pressing it between a couple of layers of paper towel with a bit of pressure.)

Whisk together the olive oil, soy sauce, garlic, and vinegar. Place the marinade in a bowl or plastic bag, along with the pressed tofu. Let marinate for at least 30 minutes and up to 6 hours.

Preheat the oven to 325°F.

Remove the tofu from the marinade, place it in a baking dish in one layer, and roast it until the tofu has a firm texture and has a caramelized color to it, about 40 minutes.

✱ When you go to the store, tofu will likely be sold as silken, regular, firm, extra-firm, and super-firm. Silken is custard-like and super-firm is sliceable, an almost meat-like consistency. When you buy it for general use you are most likely trying to keep its shape and texture, and I would recommend firm or extra-firm.

† Tofu is a bit like a sponge; pressing it expels the flavorless water from the inside, then marinating it allows it to reabsorb flavor.

GRILLED CHEESE

WHY DO I WANT TO MAKE THIS?

I remember the first food I made was paprika grilled cheese toasts. I was four. I also remember eating at my friend Sam Butler's house when I was six. His mother made us simple grilled cheeses with a little pile of ketchup to dip the sandwiches into. I never ate like that at my house so it was kind of like heaven.

You should know how to make something that has nourished us since we grew teeth. It is just a simple comfort food and well, now more than ever, we need those types of things. So learn to do it right—with just the right balance of ooze and crunch.

WHY DO I WANT TO LEARN TO MAKE THIS?

Doing this well will teach you how to not burn butter, pan-toast perfectly, and get a meltingly good result. It is the perfect rainy day lunch, ready in under 6 minutes. And from that basic point, you can riff and add stuff to make it yours—a teaspoon of minced onions in the cheese? How about some ham, leftover pulled pork, and pickles? Anything goes.

HOW DO I MAKE THIS DIFFERENT?

Add apple butter and prosciutto.

Use a new cheese: Gouda, Gruyère, tomme, mozzarella . . .

Add roasted peppers, olives, and basil.

Think about what goes with cheese and bread! Try it!

Add some pesto to the unbuttered side of the bread before you add cheese.

Use it as a base for poached eggs (page 25) with dressed greens.

Add some Slow-Roasted Onions (page 59) and maybe some slices of pear.

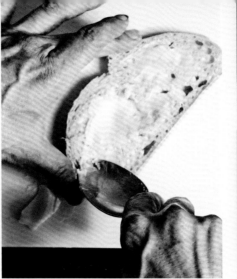

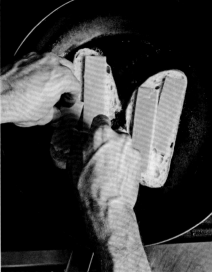

How Do I Make This?

GRILLED CHEESE
SERVES 1

1 tablespoon unsalted butter, softened *

2 slices sourdough bread †

3 ounces sliced medium cheddar cheese ‡, or whatever cheese you like

Butter one side of each of the bread slices §. Set a large skillet over medium or medium-low heat and when it is hot, place the bread butter-side down in the pan. Evenly distribute the cheese over the bread. Let the bread toast until golden brown, 3 to 5 minutes, depending on your stove and pan, occasionally peeking to see how the advancement to golden is progressing. The cheese will begin to melt, and once the bread is golden, make the sandwich by . . . okay, you know how to make a sandwich. (If you're adding ingredients, now is the time to do it: With both slices still in the pan, put the added ingredients on only one of the slices, then flip the other slice of bread cheese-side down on top of it.) Reduce the heat to low and cook 1 more minute on one side and then 1 minute on the other, to let the cheese fully melt. Remove from the pan and eat.

---

* "Softened" butter just means letting it sit outside the fridge for a few minutes until it's easily spreadable.

† I love sourdough because the tanginess balances the richness of the cheese, but use what you like. Some fancy-pants chefs will swear by brioche, levain, or other breads, but tried-and-true sourdough is what I use.

‡ I like medium cheddar. It melts well and is a classic. American cheese is fine—I adore it on a burger, but up your game with the cheddar.

§ The butter is on the outside of the sandwich, and will help the bread toast to a golden brown, because fat/oil/butter helps to evenly distribute the heat from the pan onto your food.

SLOW-ROASTED ONIONS

WHY DO I WANT TO MAKE THIS?

Onions start out raw and repellent (though I have a soft spot for a little shaved raw onion on a sandwich or in a salad) but transform, through gentle cooking, into sweet things that even a toddler adores. These super simple slow-roasted onions, so soft they're almost melted and sugar-sweet, are like gold in your kitchen. It takes a little while to make, but you don't have to do anything, and you can use their satisfying flavor in so many dishes. You can top a steak with them, chop them and scramble them with eggs, pile them on a grilled cheese, or put them on a shaved turkey sandwich, not to mention adding them to soups, sauces, or stews. They can be a staple in your fridge you can rely on for a punch of flavor.

WHY DO I WANT TO LEARN TO MAKE THIS?

The technique of low-and-slow roasting is transformative for onions, but you can also make roasted garlic the same way. (You can skip the butter, use a splash of olive oil, and start checking on them in about 40 minutes.) And it can work for so many dense, hard vegetables, like carrots.

HOW DO I USE THIS?

Chop them finely and add them to scrambled eggs.

Top toasts with roasted onions and shaved Stilton or other strong cheese.

Toss penne with roasted onions, marinara, and fresh mozzarella and bake.

Pair them with roasted chicken and green goddess dressing or vinaigrette.

Use a blender to puree them into a sauce with a touch of cream to make a soubise for Strip Steak, Onion Puree, and Spinach (page 180).

Combine with oranges, dill, and butter lettuce in an exemplary salad of big bold flavors.

Sauté fresh peas and finish with chopped roasted onions and a dollop of Greek yogurt.

Stew them with some chickpeas and chicken broth, with thinly sliced collard greens.

Have some toast with bacon, Poached Eggs (page 25), chopped roasted onions, and Red Sofrito (page 67).

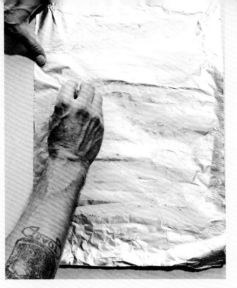

How Do I Make This?

SLOW-ROASTED ONIONS
MAKES 4 CUPS

2 sweet onions ✳, each about the size of a baseball

2 tablespoons cold unsalted butter, cubed

Kosher salt

1 tablespoon cider vinegar

4 or 5 sprigs of fresh thyme †

Preheat the oven to 325°F.

Slice a bit of the root off the bottom of the onions, but try to keep the thick root part of the onion intact so the onion petals all stay attached. Repeat with the top of the onions, taking just the bare minimum off. Peel away the skin of the onions. Quarter them from top to bottom.

Place a 2-foot length of foil on the counter and rub with some of the butter. Place the cut onions on the buttered foil, season with a couple pinches of salt, drizzle with the cider vinegar, and dot the onions with the remaining butter. Place the thyme on the onions and then fold over the sides to envelope and crimp to seal.

Place the foil-wrapped onions on a sheet pan and bake for 1½ hours. They should feel very soft through the foil. Allow to cool for 1 hour in their foil before unwrapping. Unwrap, discard the thyme sprigs, and use right away or pack in a sealable container with the juices at the bottom of the foil pouch; you can add it to any sauce or pasta. These will keep in the fridge for up to 1 week in a sealed container.

✳ Near my home is the American capital of the onion, Vidalia. I am prone to buying these. Walla Walla onions from Washington are beautiful and packed with sweetness. Texas sweet onions are a storied species, dubbed the Million Dollar Baby for their role in making onions the leading agricultural product of the state. Maui sweet onions from Hawaii are legendary as well. But you can also use regular white or yellow onions.

† I love the woodsy flavor of fresh thyme, especially with butter and onions. If you don't like it, or don't have it, make the onions without it.

ROASTED VEGETABLES

WHY Do I WANT To MAKE This?

When people say they don't like vegetables, the first thing you should feed them is good roasted vegetables. In the previous building block, we slow-roasted onions; here we will hard-roast vegetables to get intense flavors, crispy bits, and caramelized sugars. You can use these in a salad, in a pasta, or in a brothy soup, or as a stand-alone side. And you can take them any way you want, flavorwise, by tossing on some simple ingredients when they're ready—crunchy nuts, dried fruits, shaved cheeses, garlic oil, chile oils, vinaigrettes . . .

WHY Do I WANT To LEARN To MAKE This?

This core technique is really flexible and you can adjust it to just about any vegetable. It's a modern go-to, and it's easy—it requires little more than some cutting and scattering on a roasting pan. Once you get the method down—and you'll get it down after doing it once—you can experiment with pretty much anything.

How Do I USE This or MAKE It Even TASTIER?

Roasted cauliflower with grated Parmesan and toasted almonds

Roasted carrots with butter and fresh thyme leaves

Roasted broccoli with capers, raisins, chiles, and lemon zest

Roasted eggplant with tahini and za'atar spice

Roasted Brussels sprouts with lime juice and toasted peanuts

Roasted leeks with quartered hard-boiled eggs and vinaigrette

Roasted vegetables of any kind with chiles and with any of the Super Simple Sauces (pages 84 to 87): nuoc cham, cucumber raita, salsa rossa, or salsa verde

Roasted cabbage slices with vinaigrette (with some roasted peppers pureed into it)

Roasted pumpkin goes great in many soups to give them heft.

Roasted vegetable tacos with cheese or scrambled eggs and salsa

How Do I Make This?

ROASTED BROCCOLI
SERVES 2 TO 4

1 head broccoli (1 to 1½ pounds) or other hardy vegetables ✳

1 teaspoon Diamond Crystal kosher salt, or ½ teaspoon Morton kosher salt

3 tablespoons olive oil

Arrange an oven rack in the bottom third of the oven and preheat the oven to 425°F †.

Cut off the bottom inch of the broccoli stalk and compost it. Use the same knife or a vegetable peeler to peel away the tough skin of the rest of the stem ‡. Cut away the florets of the broccoli into a bowl. Slice the stem into ¼- to ½-inch-thick slices and add to the bowl. Toss well with the salt and olive oil. Spread them out in one layer on a sheet pan with some space between them §.

Transfer to the oven and roast until well toasted, about 15 minutes. You will hear sizzling; when you smell nice browned smells, take a look. If the edges are charred crispy, they should be done.

✳ Try roots like potatoes, sweet potatoes, or carrots; onions or leeks; sturdy greens like bok choy and broccolini; pumpkins, peeled, seeded, and cubed, or any other winter squash; asparagus; or cauliflower, Brussels sprouts, or cabbage (which are all cousins of broccoli—the brassica family).

† If you are using this method for other vegetables, you can play a little with the temperature and time. General rule: the hotter the oven, the more caramelization in shorter time, but the easier it is to burn. So just check on the stuff a little more carefully, or go cooler, like 400°F, and wait a little longer.

‡ The broccoli stem is delicious, sweet, and denser than the florets. You do have to peel the outside, or it can be tough. Cut it smaller to let it cook at the same rate. If you're using other veg, aim for 1-inch-ish bite-size pieces.

§ This is called "not crowding the pan," which gives hot air more room to cook each piece. If they are all piled up, they will steam, not roast.

WHY DO I WANT TO MAKE THIS?

I am not your parent, so you don't need me to tell you to eat your greens. But look: Greens are incredibly good for you. They taste great, especially when sautéed with garlic and onions as here, and finished with a little butter. Once you get a taste for them you will always want them. They're easy to cook in minutes, are a good value at the store, can be gussied up in many ways, and can complete a meal. Gotta eat your veggies, right?

WHY DO I WANT TO LEARN TO MAKE THIS?

This method of cooking greens is like stir-fry 101. Think of it like that. Get comfortable with this technique and you can use it on most greens, or julienned zucchini, sliced peppers, strips of chicken breast, anything that can cook quickly. High heat and relatively constant stirring in the pan are the keys here.

HOW DO I USE THIS OR MAKE IT EVEN TASTIER?

Make a brothy soup and finish it with sautéed greens.

Pair sautéed greens with roasted chicken.

Add more butter and a splash of heavy cream or dollop of crème fraîche and eat with steak.

Add feta cheese and some cumin near the end of cooking.

Eat them straight up.

Put them on buttery toast.

Add minced ginger and a shot of soy sauce near the end of cooking.

Fold them into scrambled eggs.

How Do I Make This?

GARLIC SAUTÉED SWISS CHARD
SERVES 2 TO 4

1 bunch Swiss chard or other greens

2 tablespoons extra-virgin olive oil

5 medium shallots or 1 small onion, thinly sliced

2 garlic cloves, minced

Pinch of red pepper flakes

½ teaspoon Diamond Crystal kosher salt, or a nice pinch of Morton kosher salt

1 teaspoon unsalted butter

Strip the leafy greens from their stems *. Cut the stems finely and tear the leaves into big pieces. Fill a large bowl with cold water †. Stir the greens and stems in the water. Let them settle for a couple minutes, then lift them out. Drain the bowl and rinse out any grit that remains. Repeat this process until no grit remains. Place the greens on towels to absorb excess water ‡.

In a large skillet, heat 1 tablespoon olive oil over high heat. When the oil starts to shimmer, add the shallots and cook until translucent. Add the garlic and cook for 1 minute. Add the pepper flakes and stir well. Scrape this mixture into a small bowl.

Wipe out the pan, return to high heat, and add 1 tablespoon olive oil. Once it shimmers, add the greens. Be careful as the oil may splatter. Cook, stirring frequently, for about 3 minutes. The greens will cook down a lot in volume. Add the shallot mixture. Season with salt. Stir and cook for 1 minute, stirring in the butter at the end, just until melted.

---

* If your greens are tender, like spinach, you don't need to separate the leaves from the stems. Or for something like bok choy that is mostly stem, just chop up the whole thing.

† Sometimes greens come prewashed. Sometimes they come with grit still on them. Check them thoroughly. If there is absolutely no grit, skip the washing step, or just give them a quick rinse.

‡ Make sure the greens are not wet when they go into the pan. This will encourage sautéing.

GREENS YOU SHOULD SAUTÉ
Use this method to sauté any of the following:

KALE   Do not hate kale because someone told you it is a passing fad. Kale is great raw, braised, or cooked fast like this on high heat, but slice it fine and give it a couple more minutes in the pan. Taste as you cook—it should be tender but pleasantly chewy.

SPINACH   Cooks faster than any green. But loses volume like a popped balloon, so cook a huge mound of it. Loves garlic and butter.

BEET GREENS   Needs a bit longer to cook than spinach. Bitter if underdone. Really good for you. Separate leaves from stems and chop the stems finely.

ROMAINE   Yeah, it is lettuce, but it cooks well. Also likes to be grilled.

ICEBERG   Gets no respect, but I do love it. It is amazing when chopped and sautéed.

CABBAGE   For faster cook times, use thin-leafed cabbages, like Savoy or napa. Great flavor.

WATERCRESS   Terrific peppery flavor. Chop the stems finely and add them, too.

BOK CHOY   Size varies. For large varieties, separate leaves from stems and chop the stems finely.

BROCCOLI RABE   Takes a few more minutes to cook than other greens. Has a pronounced bitter, peppery flavor that I love.

MUSTARD GREENS   Pungent but wonderful. They pack a wallop of heat sometimes, so taste them as you cook them.

TURNIP GREENS   One of my personal favorites. Loves a speedy cook with a good amount of butter. Also loves soy sauce and sesame.

SLAW: SIMPLE AND CLASSIC

Why Do I Want To Make This?

The flavors of this coleslaw are comforting, familiar, and timeless: caraway, dill, and cider vinegar. This version replaces half the mayo with low-fat plain yogurt. This makes it a much healthier slaw than many slaws of yore.

But you can also make a super simple slaw with just salt, pepper, oil, and vinegar, and taste the fresh crunch and sweetness of the cabbage that you can take in any direction you want.

Slaw is easy and makes a meal complete.

Why Do I Want To Learn To Make This?

Cabbage gets a bad rap: People think it's ho-hum or, at worst, boiled and stinky. But a head of cabbage is something you want to keep in your fridge, because unlike many greens, it can last a good long time, so you can have a fresh vegetable side or salad on hand anytime. And when you make slaw yourself you control the flavors and the richness, so it doesn't have to be the monotony of cabbage and mayo that you often find.

The key to slaw is a soak in icy salt water, after you have shredded it. This changes the cell structure of the cabbage and makes it very crunchy.

After that, it's really up to you how you want to go with the dressing. You can literally just oil and vinegar it like a simple salad, use the classic-tasting mayo/yogurt dressing at right, or add herbs, other vegetables, or other flavors to it. It's a great canvas.

Or use the method and replace some or all of the cabbage with:
- shredded carrots
- broccoli leaves (some grocery stores just sell bags of leaves now)
- fresh fennel, apples, and cabbage together

How Do I Use This / How Do I Riff on This?

Make it with a pinch of cayenne, olive oil, and freshly squeezed lime juice.

Top tacos with it.

Lose the mayo entirely and sub in olive oil.

Good slaw's crunch and freshness is such a great go-to accompaniment to pretty much anything.

Put it next to some roasted chicken and rice.

Serve it with some Slow-Roasted Pork Shoulder (page 48), hot sauce, and corn bread.

Use it on a sandwich, any sandwich (okay, maybe not PB&J).

In a collard greens sandwich (it's a Southern thing)

Put it *on* a burger, not just beside it.

Serve it with anything fried.

How Do I Make This?

CLASSIC SLAW
SERVES 4

1 medium head green cabbage

Kosher salt

½ cup plain low-fat yogurt

¼ cup mayonnaise

3 tablespoons cider vinegar

1 teaspoon toasted caraway seeds

¼ teaspoon freshly ground black pepper

1 tablespoon fresh lime juice

½ cup finely sliced scallions

½ cup minced peeled celery

¼ cup finely minced flat-leaf parsley

1 tablespoon chopped fresh dill

Halve the cabbage from top to bottom, through the root core. Cut the core out of each half—it's thick and dense rather than leafy—and then finely slice the rest of the cabbage with a knife. Take your time. No one with four fingers is glad they rushed that project in which they lost a digit.

Place the cabbage in a bowl and toss with 2 tablespoons kosher salt. Cover with ice water and let sit for 1 hour. (This is for the best slaw; you can skip if you don't have the time.)

Drain the cabbage and lay it out on a kitchen towel to get rid of excess moisture. At this point you can refrigerate it to dress later, even a few days from now.

Place the cabbage in a large bowl.

In a small bowl, combine the yogurt, mayonnaise, vinegar, caraway, pepper, and lime juice. Season the dressing with salt to taste. Then add the scallions, celery, parsley, and dill. Add the dressing to the cabbage, toss to coat, adjust the seasoning with more salt, if desired, and put it on the table.

SUPER SIMPLE VERSION
Omit all the ingredients except the cabbage and 1 teaspoon salt. After you have salted the cabbage in the bowl, dress it with cider vinegar and extra-virgin olive oil to taste. Add anything else you want, if you want it.

WHY Do I WANT To MAKE THIS?

Sofrito is a flavor bomb that is added to many dishes in Spain, Portugal, and the Caribbean. (Italians have their own versions as well.) It is a mixture of onions, peppers, tomatoes, and spices, cooked down to a thick, flavor-packed paste. It is a base to use for a sauce or stew. You can spread it on toast. You can slather a piece of chicken with it. You can use it as a condiment. It is something to lean on and deserves a place in your fridge.

Traditionally, the ingredients change from place to place, and are sometimes cooked and sometimes not. You will see green sofritos as well, but this one is inspired by the red Spanish sofrito that is the base of great paella.

WHY Do I WANT To LEARN To MAKE THIS?

I love this recipe—it is really a beautiful flavor—but the technique is what's important for you here. You can mix and match or omit or add ingredients as you like, but the method of slow-cooking first onions and garlic, and then other flavorful, saucy vegetables until they've cooked off their water and become almost pasty, will result in so many delicious things for you. They become that key component that you can rely on.

How Do I USE This?

Quickly stewed fresh or frozen peas with chicken broth, sofrito, and pulled roasted chicken

Finish a stew with a big spoonful of it.

Stir it into softened butter for a simple compound butter to spread on things.

Stir it into a mayonnaise for a dip or sandwich spread.

Dollop onto grilled scallions or other vegetables.

Stew cucumber in sofrito and finish with minced parsley.

Slather it on bread for a chicken sandwich with mayo and lettuce.

Sauté ground beef until browned, stir in some sofrito, and make tacos with cabbage slaw.

Hash Browns (page 32) with sofrito and sautéed spinach

Thin it out with chicken stock and stew chicken in it.

Use as a sauce for asparagus with grated hard-boiled egg.

Poached Eggs with Sofrito, Buttered Kale, and Grits (page 181)

It is a huge flavor to finish simply cooked rice. Add some roasted tofu (page 55).

How Do I Make This?

RED SOFRITO
MAKES ABOUT 3 CUPS

2 tablespoons extra-virgin olive oil
1 medium onion, small diced
2 garlic cloves, minced *
2 shallots, minced
1 teaspoon paprika
4 ounces canned diced green chiles
2 roasted red bell peppers, chopped †
1 (28-ounce) can chopped tomatoes, drained
½ cup chicken or vegetable stock
Kosher salt

In a large skillet, heat the olive oil over medium heat. Once the oil is hot, add the onion, garlic, and shallots. Stir often as it cooks to prevent burning at the bottom of the pan. Cook until the onions are very soft and starting to get golden, about 12 minutes.

Add the paprika and cook for 2 more minutes. Add the green chiles, roasted red peppers, tomatoes, and chicken stock. Bring the mixture to a boil, reduce to a simmer, and cook until reduced and almost dry, about 30 minutes. Season with salt to taste. You want the consistency to be like a thick tomato sauce. It is meant to be a powerful flavor concentrate to add to dishes later on. Cool it well, pack it up, and use it a lot.

I store sofrito in a clean container in the fridge for up to a week, and use it in all sorts of things. Or freeze it in small quantities (in an ice cube tray, then popped out into plastic bags works great) for later use.

---

* "Minced" just means it should be very finely chopped into tiny bits.

† You can buy these in jars, but they are best when you make them yourself. Put the whole, raw peppers right on a gas burner or under the broiler turned to high, turning with tongs as soon as one side is blackened. When they are blackened all over, put them in a bowl and seal with plastic wrap. This will help steam off the skins. Peel and wipe away the skins, rinsing the peppers a touch if needed. Break them open and cut out the seeds and stem.

ROASTED CHICKEN

WHY Do I Want To Make This?

Nothing says "real cooking" like a good roasted chicken—juicy, with beautifully browned skin. For chefs, it's a benchmark of how good a cook you are, because it's so simple, but royally screwed up by so many. But for home cooks, it's just about a few simple tricks to make sure you nail it and, more important, that you have something delicious to feed yourself with—as well as leftovers you can use later on to make sandwiches, stews, pastas, soups, chicken salad, chicken stock, etc.

WHY Do I Want To LEARN To Make This?

Learning how to put a beautifully roasted chicken on the table means you have gained a life skill. It's like the difference between just learning how to play chess and actually being good at chess.

How Do I Make This?

ROASTED CHICKEN
SERVES 2 TO 4 (OR 1 WITH LOTS OF LEFTOVERS)

1 whole chicken (3 to 4 pounds)
1 tablespoon plus 1 teaspoon Diamond Crystal kosher salt, or 2½ teaspoons Morton kosher salt
2 tablespoons canola or other oil
1 teaspoon baking powder
1 tablespoon fresh thyme leaves (optional)

DAY BEFORE   Take out the package of giblets and trim any large pieces of fat. Salt the bird all over and inside the cavity with 1 tablespoon of the salt (or the 2 teaspoons). Leave it uncovered on a large plate or a baking dish on a lower shelf of the refrigerator and make sure it doesn't bump into other food. Let it sit in the fridge until you're ready to cook the next day ✳.

DAY OF   Preheat the oven to 450°F. Pat the chicken dry with paper towels. Cross the chicken legs at the last joint and tie them together with twine †.

Use a brush to coat the chicken with 1 tablespoon of the oil. Mix together the remaining 1 teaspoon (or ½ teaspoon) salt and baking powder (make sure it's not baking soda, which will lead to an unpleasant taste) in a small bowl. Season the chicken all over with this mixture ‡.

Place the chicken on a sheet pan or cast-iron skillet and roast for 30 minutes. Using towels or mitts, take the pan out of the oven and reduce the oven temperature to 375°F. Brush the skin with the remaining 1 tablespoon oil and sprinkle with thyme (if using). Return the chicken to the oven and roast until the thickest part of the breast reads 155° to 160°F on a meat thermometer §, about another 20 minutes. Remove it from the oven and let it rest 20 minutes before carving ¶.

✳ Presalting will help crisp the skin and season the meat all the way through.

† Tying the legs together helps give the bird an even shape, so it cooks evenly.

‡ The baking powder creates a chemical reaction with the skin and helps it brown much more evenly and deeply.

§ Get a thermometer. They're cheap and it's way better to use that than to guess whether meat is done or overcooked. The USDA says to cook poultry to 160°F for it to be safe, or 155°F if you can keep it at that temperature for 5 minutes. Since there is residual heat in the food that "carries over"—meaning the internal temperature will still go up a couple of degrees after you take it out of the oven—155°F is probably going to be fine.

¶ Resting meats after cooking is key; it lets the juices settle back into the meat instead of running out when you cut it.

CARVING A CHICKEN

Pull the thigh away from the body and cut through the skin and joint to remove the leg. Slice down just off center of the breast; the knife will hit cartilage. Angle the knife to carve off the breast. Press hard to cut through the wing joint. Slice the breast against the grain, then cut through the joint between the thigh and leg.

How Do I Use This?

After you've picked all the usable meat from the carcass, boil and then simmer the carcass in water, with some onion, celery, and carrot, and you have chicken stock for chicken soup.

Leftover chicken can be used to make fried rice. Just sub it in for the pork in Fried Rice with Pork and Kimchi (page 114).

The best meal in my house is simple: Roasted Chicken with Radicchio, Capers, Eggplant, and Crisp Bread (page 189).

Pick any leftover meat off the bones, chop it, and use it to make chicken salad, such as Roasted Chicken Salad (page 202).

Make roasted chicken sandwiches with mayo, lettuce, and cheese.

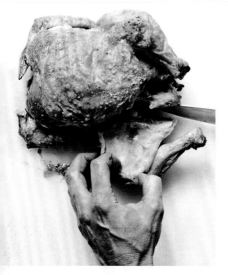

WHY DO I WANT TO MAKE THIS?

Of all the dishes in the world, steak is probably the one I least need to convince most people to make. I love steak, too, which is why I'd rather get a great steak and splurge on it occasionally, and just eat less of it or eat it less often. A great steak is more expensive, yes, but tastes much better, and one good steak can serve two or more people. If you love steak, too, this is how you should make it. We'll get a beautiful crust on a steak that is nice and thick, and we'll cook correctly.

WHY DO I WANT TO LEARN TO MAKE THIS?

There are two methods shown here: One is all on the stovetop, where you sear the steak, then use a generous bath of hot butter to continuously baste the steak; this speeds things up, gets a better crust, and gives you control throughout the cooking process. The other is a two-stage cook, where you sear the steak in a pan and then finish cooking it in the oven; the oven helps to cook the steak evenly, and as long as you pull it out in time you'll have good results.

In both cases, you'll want a meat thermometer to tell you how well your meat is cooked.

You can also use these methods to make pork or lamb chops, chicken or duck breasts or thighs, or sausages.

HOW DO I USE THIS?

Accompany steak with some sautéed greens (see page 63).

Make a steak sandwich.

Accompany the steak with roasted vegetables (see page 61).

Strip Steak, Onion Puree, and Spinach (page 180)

Steak Salad with Green Papaya (page 193)

Top a steak with Sautéed Mushrooms (page 31).

Top a steak with a poached egg (see page 25).

Steak Salad with Pickled Radishes and Soy Vinaigrette (page 215)

How Do I Make This?

BUTTER-BASTED OR PAN-ROASTED STEAK
SERVES 2

1 New York strip steak **✳**, 1 to 1½ inches thick (12 to 16 ounces)

1 teaspoon Diamond Crystal kosher salt, or ½ teaspoon Morton kosher salt

Freshly ground black pepper

1 tablespoon canola oil

4 tablespoons unsalted butter (skip if pan-roasting), cut into chunks and chilled

4 to 6 fresh thyme and rosemary sprigs (skip if pan-roasting)

Season the steak all over with the salt. Set on a plate and let rest uncovered, ideally for at least 1 hour in the fridge. (If you have time to let it rest overnight, that's best.)

TO BUTTER-BASTE Remove the steak from the fridge 30 minutes before you will be cooking it. Pat the steak very dry with paper towels and season with black pepper. Heat a heavy 10-inch skillet **†** over high heat. When the pan is super hot, after a few minutes of heating, add the oil; it should smoke quickly. Immediately lay in the steak gently **‡**. Don't touch the steak. Let the pan do the work **§**.

Cook until a beautiful golden brown crust has formed, 2 or 3 minutes. Turn the steak over with tongs and sear for another 2 minutes. Reduce the heat to medium, add the butter, thyme, and rosemary and baste the bubbling butter over the steak with a small serving spoon. To make the basting easier, hold the pan handle with a kitchen towel and tilt the pan a little toward yourself to pool the butter.

Baste continuously for 1 minute and then turn the steak over. Baste for another minute and check the internal temperature with a meat thermometer, sticking it in the center of the thickness of the steak: 120°F is rare, 125°F is

medium-rare, 135°F is medium, 145°F is medium-well, and 150°F is well-done. Keep cooking and basting and turning every minute to get to your desired doneness.

Remove the steak to a platter to rest for 5 minutes. Transfer to a clean cutting board and look at the grain of the meat, which means which direction the muscle fibers run in. You want to cut against that grain to slice the steak; shorter fibers means more tender bites.

TO PAN-ROAST Preheat the oven to 425°F. Taking care to use an ovenproof skillet, follow the method as above, but after the initial sear, flip the steak and pop the pan in the oven. Take the pan out and check the temperature after 5 minutes; continue cooking it in the oven if necessary. DON'T FORGET ABOUT IT! For a lot of cooks, the oven makes you forget what you were doing, kind of the bad results version of "out of sight, out of mind."

✳ This can also be a rib eye, tenderloin (filet mignon), or other cuts or meats—like pork chops or chicken parts—you like. When you are shopping for a steak, look for brilliant red, a good amount of streaky fat within the meat (called marbling), and not much tough, silvery sinew.

† I like a cast-iron or heavy stainless skillet. It should be about 10 inches in diameter, not much bigger, because the oil will just burn in the pointless acreage of a huge pan.

‡ Don't drop it in. Lay it in gently, so the oil doesn't splash on you.

§ Don't be tempted to move the meat around; let it cook to get good color.

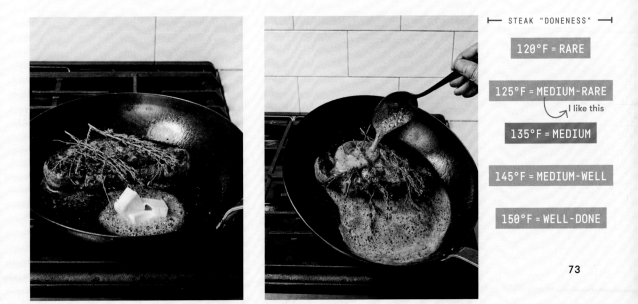

├─ STEAK "DONENESS" ─┤

120°F = RARE

125°F = MEDIUM-RARE
    ↳ I like this

135°F = MEDIUM

145°F = MEDIUM-WELL

150°F = WELL-DONE

WHY DO I WANT TO MAKE THIS?

Fish is a delicious, lean protein, and what fat it does have is the best kind of fat for you—fish fat is brain food. Cooking fish seems to confound many people. Fish is expensive and to cook it badly is a risky use of funds, so let's cook it well. Think about a good sear, a tender center, and warm through. When it comes to cooking the most ubiquitous fish available, I want to have salmon skin as crisp as a chip, with beautiful, juicy, pink flesh underneath. And you can make it, I promise.

WHY DO I WANT TO LEARN TO MAKE THIS?

Cooking fish can be intimidating, but this technique becomes pretty idiotproof after you've done it once or twice. The fish just needs to be fresh, dry to the touch before it goes in the pan, and seasoned well. The rest kind of takes care of itself. If you are worried about it sticking to the pan, you can always use a nonstick pan, but even a regular pan will work if you get it nice and hot before cooking.

Once you learn to cook the salmon (as opposite), you can branch out to other fish: halibut, cod, sole, snapper, grouper, or trout are easily accessible fish that can be bought at most grocers.

The recipe calls for skin-on fillets, but if you have skinless fish, NO BIGGIE. That just means that you will flip the fish sooner and cook it more evenly on both sides.

HOW DO I USE THIS?

Salmon with shaved radishes and sauced with miso vinaigrette (take the vinaigrette on page 27 and stir miso into it, to taste)

Butter lettuce salad with chopped roasted vegetables (see page 61) and pan-roasted salmon

Fettuccine with roasted salmon, crème fraîche, and scallions

Seared Catfish with Chile-Tomato-Coconut Broth (page 208)

Pan-roasted salmon with celery and apple salad on top

Pan-roasted halibut with sofrito-infused chickpeas (see pages 67 and 44)

Pan-roasted salmon on a toasted bagel with cream cheese and dill

Pan-roasted salmon served with sautéed spinach (see page 63) and mashed cooked white beans (see page 44)

Salmon with roasted beets (see roasted vegetables on page 61), and a dollop of dilled sour cream

How Do I Make This?

PAN-ROASTED SALMON
SERVES 2

2 skin-on salmon fillets (6 ounces each), about ¾ inch thick *

Kosher salt

1 tablespoon canola oil

A few sprigs fresh dill (optional)

Lemon wedges (optional)

Freshly ground black pepper

Using paper towels, pat the salmon dry on both sides †. Lightly season the fillets all over with salt. Heat a heavy-bottomed skillet ‡ over medium-high heat with the canola oil in it. Wait for the oil to shimmer.

Gently lay the salmon in the pan, skin-side down. Reduce the heat to medium-low. Using a spatula or a long spoon, gently press down on the fish as soon as it hits the pan; this keeps the skin flat and crispy. Press for 10 or 15 seconds, until the fish no longer wants to buckle upward.

Cook the salmon through most of the way on the skin side (this is the way to go; it helps prevent overcooking the fillet). The skin should release easily from the pan after 4 minutes of cooking; keep it on there for another minute or two for more crispness, then flip it and cook for another minute or so.

Insert a meat thermometer into the middle of the thickness: 125° to 130°F for medium; 140°F if you like more cooked-through fish. (These temperatures will work for most all fish, but fish like swordfish and halibut like to be cooked through, so lean toward the 140°F.) Here is another trick: Total cooking time should be 8 minutes for every inch of thickness at the thickest point of the fish.

Serve with some snips of fresh dill, a squeeze of lemon, and definitely a little freshly ground black pepper.

* Fresh usually has advantages over frozen. Frozen fish often retains a lot of moisture and can wick that wetness into the pan as you cook it, sogging up the crust. Find a place that sells a lot of fish and you will have better results. And if sustainability of our oceans means a lot to you, as it does to me, then look up your fish choices on Seafood Watch, an online resource that grades where fish comes from and whether it is on its last legs or fins.

† Any moisture that we can remove from the exterior of the fish fillet is going to help it sear rather than steam.

‡ Nonstick is great if you're nervous about the fish sticking, but if you get the pan very hot before cooking, you shouldn't need it.

WHY DO I WANT TO MAKE THIS?

What is more comforting than a warm bowl of soft cornmeal porridge? If that doesn't sound so great, we can use its more common names: polenta or grits. In the South, where I live, a bowl of buttered grits with eggs is a classic breakfast. In Italy, polenta topped with braised meats is a classic. Whatever you want to call it, a hearty porridge of cornmeal cooked with water, stock, or milk until it's tender is a vehicle for so many wonderful dishes. You can add sautéed mushrooms, wilted greens, a poached egg, or some braised chicken. It is a vehicle for flavors, or a pleasure all on its own, with some butter and grated Parmesan.

WHY DO I WANT TO LEARN TO MAKE THIS?

The method for making porridge is pretty similar across most grains; the biggest difference is usually going to come down to how much liquid you use and how long you cook it. The ratio I use is 1 part cornmeal to 5 parts liquid for a soft polenta, and 1 part cornmeal to 4 parts liquid for a polenta that I will cook and then pour into a baking dish and set to a firm texture in the fridge. Then you can cut it and sauté it in a pan or grill it for a great accompaniment. These same ratios can be used for stoneground hominy grits. ("Quick" and "instant" grits are not in my wheelhouse, but they have directions on their respective boxes.)

HOW DO I USE THIS?

Roasted Chicken and Grits with Broth and Poached Eggs (page 92)

Buttery cheddar cheese grits with roasted broccoli

Polenta with Italian sausage, oregano, and Parmesan on top

Shrimp and grits

Steak with a side of polenta and Salsa Rossa (page 84)

Top polenta with Sautéed Mushrooms (page 31).

Sautéed firm polenta, served with Red Sofrito (page 67)

Stir parsley, garlic, and Fontina cheese into polenta.

How Do I Make This?

SOFT POLENTA OR GRITS
SERVES 4 TO 6

5 cups water, stock, or milk (or a combination)
1 cup cornmeal (not corn flour) or grits ✱
Kosher salt
2 tablespoons unsalted butter
Grated Parmesan cheese †, lots (optional)

This is an optional step, but presoaking the cornmeal/grits helps the polenta or grits cook more quickly. To do this: Combine the water, cornmeal/grits, and 2 teaspoons kosher salt and let soak at room temperature for 8 hours or so. (In the fridge if you're using any stock or milk.)

Transfer the mixture to a large saucepan or heavy-bottomed pot ‡ and bring to a boil over medium-high heat, stirring frequently, being sure to scrape all over the bottom of the pot. Cook until the mixture thickens. Reduce the heat and continue to cook gently, stirring often § until the mixture becomes thick enough to pull away from sides of the pot,

about 30 minutes for polenta, and about an hour for grits.

Give the polenta/grits a taste. The polenta should be smooth and creamy with no lumps. The grits, which are coarse-ground, will be a little rougher in texture. Season with salt if necessary and whisk in the butter until fully incorporated. Stir in the grated Parmesan, if using. Serve immediately.

✱ Most any kind of cornmeal will work. *Do not use corn flour, though.* That will become glue. Bramata is an Italian cornmeal I love for polenta. Grits have a coarser grind and end up, well, a little gritty—but in a good way.

† Or use other cheeses—cheddar is typical for grits.

‡ Heavy-bottomed pots and pans even out the heat from the burner better, so are less likely to burn your food.

§ It's important to agitate the bottom of the pot to prevent the polenta or grits from sticking to the bottom of the pot and burning. Burnt polenta is the worst. You'll need to do this whenever you slow-simmer anything thick, like jam.

WHY Do I Want To Make This?

The building block recipe here is for a leek and potato soup, which in French sounds fancy: vichyssoise. It's classic—a creamy, smooth white soup with the sweet, gentle onion flavor of leeks. It's traditionally served cold, but it's just as great hot, and can be easily dressed up to impress. But the real reason you want to make the soup is because you will learn to puree, which is a go-to technique for many soups and sauces and the basis for a lot of great dishes.

WHY Do I Want To LEARN To Make This?

When I talk about a puree, it's usually vegetables, unless I'm making a smoothie, but I don't want to talk about smoothies right now. I want to talk about how you would use a puree. It can be a base for protein: for example, a fine carrot puree with ginger and butter served with roasted chicken and spinach. It can be pulverizing pinto beans to make your own refried beans to amaze your friends on taco night. It can become a soup of sweet leeks or onions, given body and flavor with potato. It's a basic method that can take so many foods and turn them into a great side or a foundation to build a dish, literally, on top of.

The difference between a puree as a side and a puree as a soup comes down to one thing: how much liquid you use. So if you are making a carrot puree as a side dish you would use less liquid to cook the carrots and also drain a lot of the liquid off before pureeing—only adding back enough to get to the desired consistency. For a soup, you would thin the puree with more liquid. Using the method in the soup recipe on page 80, all you have to do is swap in or out different vegetables, seasonings, and quantities of liquid—whether stock, milk, or even water—less for purees, more for soups.

HOW DO I USE THIS?

Edamame puree with feta, sumac, and preserved lemon: Boil or steam edamame beans, puree them with a little water, and top with the garnishes.

Carrot soup with ginger and shallot: Literally just sweat carrots, ginger, and shallot in butter like the leeks in this soup and proceed with the same method. Skip the potato, since carrot can thicken on its own.

Fennel puree with Roasted Chicken (page 68) and Salsa Verde (page 85)

Maple whipped sweet potatoes

Turnip puree garnished with lemon and dill and served with roasted salmon (page 75)

Strip Steak, Onion Puree, and Spinach (page 180)

Butternut Squash and Apple Soup (page 147)

Sweet Pea Soup with Yogurt and Mint (page 156)

How Do I Make This?

LEEK AND POTATO SOUP
MAKES 4 CUPS (SERVES 3 OR 4)

3 large leeks
4 tablespoons unsalted butter
Kosher salt
½ pound Yukon Gold potatoes
(1 medium)
2 cups chicken or vegetable stock
¼ teaspoon freshly ground
white pepper
1 cup heavy cream
Sliced chives or scallions, for serving

Trim off the dark green tops of the leeks, and save them for a stock if you'd like. Coarsely chop the white and light green parts, immerse them in a bowl of cold water, rinsing them of any grit that might have been hiding between the layers. Strain, and then blot them with a towel to get them pretty dry. In a large pot, melt the butter over medium heat. Add the leeks with a sprinkle of kosher salt and reduce the heat to medium-low. Stir the leeks to evenly coat with the melted butter. Keep stirring occasionally until the leeks are very soft and sweet, about 20 minutes.

Meanwhile, peel and quarter the potato and put it in a small saucepan and cover with water. Add 1 tablespoon kosher salt and bring to a boil over high heat. Reduce the heat to medium-low and simmer until just tender, about 20 minutes. Drain.

Add the chicken stock, cooked potatoes, 1 teaspoon salt, and the white pepper to the pot of tender leeks. Bring to a boil over high heat. Remove from the heat. Carefully ladle the contents of the pot into a blender ✱. Do this in batches; don't fill the blender jar more than halfway. Add half the cream. Put the blender lid on

and remove the center cap/
steam vent (or leave the lid open
a crack) †. Holding the lid in
place with an oven mitt or a towel
to protect your hand, puree on
a low speed, then increase it
to high. When it's smooth, pour
it into a bowl and repeat with
the rest of the soup and cream.
Double-check the seasoning and
add more salt and white pepper
until the flavor is great. Garnish
with chives.

You can serve this soup hot
(right away or reheated) or cold
(chilled). Store the leftovers in a
covered container in the fridge for
up to 5 days or so.

✱ You see a lot of fancy blenders on
the market these days, usually with
more horsepower than my first car.
You do not have to have a high-dollar
blender to get a great result . . . to be
honest I bought my first blender at a
garage sale for $20, and it never let
me down.

† Pureeing hot things creates steam
and pressure, which can blow the
top off your blender. That's bad. So
remove the center cap or leave the
lid open a crack so the pressure can
escape. Hold the lid in place with a
towel or mitt to protect your hand just
in case, and then blend.

WHY DO I WANT TO MAKE THIS?

When we want to ramp up the flavor in dishes, we often rely on the condiments in the door of our fridges. Here are a bunch you can make yourself that are versatile, easy to prepare, and pack a ton of flavors for lots of dishes. Three of them don't even require a stove.

One is an Italian chop-and-stir classic featuring herbs, garlic, and olive oil. Another is a salsa that isn't too far from what you'd dip tortilla chips in, but with a soft, sweet garlic oil. (Which is a sauce on its own, really.)

Then there is a 3-minute yogurt-and-cucumber sauce, so important to Indian cooking, called raita. It's rich and refreshing.

And last, a classic Vietnamese dipping sauce or dressing called nuoc cham— a mix of savory, sweet, and sour flavors. You could make many meals with a simply roasted piece of protein, rice, some lettuces, and splashes of nuoc cham.

WHY DO I WANT TO LEARN TO MAKE THESE?

All of these sauces are delicious, and can be the basis of many meals just by using them to dress or flavor simply cooked foods. But also realize they are pretty much all mix-and-matchable with flavors and ingredients you love. Like scallions? Chop them into your salsa verde. Like chile powder? Toss that in your raita. Do whatever you want; these sauces are your friends.

SALSA VERDE

Salsa verde with chicken

NUOC CHAM

Any simply cooked protein will go with any of these sauces, really.

This makes a great soup garnish. (Actually, all three sauces do, separately.)

How Do I Use This?

SALSA ROSSA

Salsa rossa with pork chop

Scrambled or poached eggs
(see page 25) with
salsa rossa and toast or
Soft Polenta (page 77)

CUCUMBER RAITA

Pita stuffed with
Pan-Roasted
Salmon (page 75),
fennel slaw, and
raita

A sauce for vegetables . . .
roasted broccoli
(see page 61)
with raita is great.

How Do I Make Them?

SALSA ROSSA
(WITH GARLIC OIL)
MAKES ABOUT 2 CUPS, PLUS
   ABOUT ¼ CUP GARLIC OIL

Italian? Spanish? Somewhere in that geographical context is salsa rossa, a condiment that's lovely on just about anything. A leftover chicken sandwich? Check. Scrambled eggs? Check. A stack of roasted tofu? Check. This does take a little bit of time because you make a garlic oil to finish it, but it's super easy, and you want to know how to make garlic oil, right? It's a condiment in its own right.

¼ cup extra-virgin olive oil

6 garlic cloves, peeled and chopped

2 plum tomatoes, diced

1 large red bell pepper, roasted (see ↑, page 67), or 8 ounces jarred roasted pepper, finely chopped

1 small red jalapeño pepper, seeded and minced

1 tablespoon chopped fresh flat-leaf parsley

1 tablespoon chopped fresh basil

Kosher salt

In a small saucepan, combine the olive oil and garlic and cook over low heat until the garlic is tender, about 30 minutes. Remove from the heat. Once cool, drain the garlic in a sieve set over a bowl. Measure out 1 tablespoon of the garlic oil and transfer to a small saucepan. (Reserve the remaining garlic oil for other uses, such as in a vinaigrette, or drizzled on rice, roasted vegetables, noodles, bread, etc. Store it in the fridge and let it come to room temp before using.)

Set the saucepan with the garlic oil over medium heat. Add the tomatoes and roasted pepper. Cook until melted, about 10 minutes. Add the garlic cloves, jalapeño, parsley, and basil. Season with salt to taste and it's done. For a smoother texture, you can puree it in a blender. Use hot or room temperature. Chill and store in the fridge for up to a week or so.

SALSA VERDE
MAKES ABOUT 2 CUPS

This is an uncooked Italian herb sauce brought together with olive oil and a splash of acid. It will keep in the fridge for about 5 days at peak freshness, but in that time can be used in many ways. Wonderful on a steak, or any simply roasted or grilled meat or fish. Also great as a quick condiment to amp up and finish a soup, pasta, or grain bowl. If you don't have or don't like one of the herbs mentioned, that's fine! It's all very loose—mix and match as you like. The anchovies give this wonderful depth (not fishiness), but skip them if you want.

½ cup packed fresh flat-leaf parsley leaves, finely chopped (about 1 bunch)

1 tablespoon finely chopped fresh basil leaves

1 tablespoon finely chopped fresh mint leaves

1 tablespoon finely chopped fresh marjoram leaves

¾ cup extra-virgin olive oil, plus more to taste

2 garlic cloves, minced

Pinch of crushed red pepper flakes

1 tablespoon salt-packed capers, rinsed well and chopped

1 tablespoon minced rinsed salt-packed anchovy fillets

1 teaspoon Dijon mustard

1 tablespoon cider vinegar

Kosher salt and freshly ground black pepper

In a medium bowl, combine the parsley, basil, mint, and marjoram and pour in the olive oil. Add the garlic, pepper flakes, capers, and anchovies. Stir well. Add the mustard and vinegar. Season with salt and pepper to taste, and thin with more olive oil if necessary. It should have the consistency of a loose pesto, but you can blend it in a blender for a smoother sauce. The salsa will keep in the refrigerator for up to 5 days.

CUCUMBER RAITA
MAKES ABOUT 2 CUPS

Raita is a staple in India, accompanying curries and rice dishes. It is a wonderfully simple sauce. Get a fast-food chicken sandwich and put raita on top—game changer. Wonderful with a simple chopped salad, poached or grilled salmon, chicken . . . very flexible.

1 cucumber

1 cup plain whole-milk yogurt

¼ teaspoon ground cumin

1 tablespoon freshly squeezed lemon juice

½ tablespoon cider vinegar

Kosher salt

Peel the cucumber and quarter it lengthwise. Scoop out the seeds with a spoon and discard. Dice the cucumber small and add to a medium bowl. Stir in the yogurt, cumin, lemon juice, cider vinegar, and salt to taste—enough salt so that you can feel the flavors brighten, but not so much that it tastes too salty. This keeps, in the fridge, for up to 1 week.

NUOC CHAM
MAKES ABOUT 2 CUPS

Nuoc cham is the wonderful Vietnamese sauce that you get with spring rolls, but do not think that the uses stop there. It is a match with rice and poached chicken, a simple salad of cucumber and tomatoes, a plate of thinly sliced seared tuna, a bowl of grilled shrimp . . . it makes food zing with acidity and umami. The fish sauce is the key, and the offsetting flavors of the sugar and the chiles. It will keep in the fridge for 1 week and takes 3 minutes to make.

1 cup hot water
½ cup sugar
½ cup freshly squeezed lime juice
⅓ cup fish sauce
1 garlic clove, finely minced
2 bird's eye chiles, thinly sliced
Kosher salt

In a small bowl, combine the hot water and sugar. Whisk to dissolve the sugar and then add lime juice, fish sauce, garlic, and chiles. Season with a pinch of salt, if necessary.

RECIPES

Now that you've learned the building blocks, let's build! Here is a sampling of recipes for you to get started.

PASTA, RICE, AND GRAINS

Spaghetti with Garlic and Olive Oil (Spaghetti Aglio e Olio) 91

Roasted Chicken and Grits with Broth and Poached Eggs 92

Gussied-Up Instant Ramen 95

Spaghetti and Meatballs 96

Louisiana-Style Dirty Rice with Greens 99

Pasta with Tomato and Cured Pork (Bucatini Amatriciana) 100

Crisped Rice with Sausage and Kimchi 103

Spaghetti with Shrimp and Leeks 104

Wheat Berry Salad with Tomato, Feta, Mint, and Olives 107

Cavatelli with Chickpeas, Tomato Sauce, Ricotta, and Basil 108

Savannah Red Rice 110

Polenta with Pork, Apples, and Slow-Roasted Onion 111

Spaghetti with Basil Pesto 113

Fried Rice with Pork and Kimchi 114

SALADS AND SANDWICHES

Chef's Salad 117

Poached Egg and Bacon Salad 118

Avocado Toast with Feta and Roasted Broccoli 120

Grilled Cheese with Pear and Slow-Cooked Onions 121

Chicken and Potato Salad with White Wine and Herbs 123

Fennel and White Bean Salad 124

Cuban Grilled Cheese 125

Iceberg Salad with Celery, Pine Nuts, and Cheese 126

Luxe Patty Melt with Slow-Roasted Onions and Pickles 128

Red Check Salad 129

Tomato, Peach, and Basil Salad 130

Spinach Salad with Pear, Pecans, Blue Cheese 133

Three-Bean Salad 134

Tomato-Crouton Salad 137

Roasted Tofu and Bacon Club Sandwich 138

Garlic-Soy Tofu Burritos 141

Fried Shrimp Po'Boys 142

Grilled Cheese with Tomato, Ham, and Slow-Cooked Onions 144

SOUPS

Rich Tomato Soup with Bread, Basil, and Olive Oil **145**

Butternut Squash and Apple Soup **147**

Portuguese Kale, Potato, and Sausage Soup (Caldo Verde) **148**

Italian Chicken Soup **151**

Black Bean Soup with Avocado and Sour Cream **152**

Smoky White Bean and Ham Soup **155**

Sweet Pea Soup with Yogurt and Mint **156**

Creamy Mushroom Soup **157**

VEGETABLES AND POTATOES

Sweet Potato and Eggs in Spicy Green Tomato Sauce (Shakshuka) **158**

Roasted Carrots with Tops, Feta, Mint, and Pickled Shallots **161**

Roasted Eggplant with Tahini, Pomegranate, Parsley, and Pecans **162**

Leeks in Sun-Dried Tomato–Olive Vinaigrette **165**

Sweet Potatoes with Tofu, Scallions, and Soy Vinaigrette **166**

Maple Sweet Potatoes with Pecans and Cheese **167**

Fingerling Potatoes with Green Garlic Vinaigrette **168**

Hash Browns with Goat Cheese and Roasted Red Peppers **170**

Hash Browns with Smoked Salmon and Things That Go with Smoked Salmon **171**

Curry Spinach and Tofu (Saag Paneer, Kinda) **173**

Seared Summer Squash with Mint and Vinaigrette **174**

Sweet Potato Hash with Salsa Rossa and Sour Cream **177**

MEAT, CHICKEN, FISH, AND EGGS

Roasted Chicken Lettuce Wraps with Herbs **178**

Strip Steak, Onion Puree, and Spinach **180**

Poached Eggs with Sofrito, Buttered Kale, and Grits **181**

Steak with Hash Browns, Mushrooms, and Warm Vinaigrette **182**

Salmon and Lemon-Mint Rice with Raita and Lettuces **185**

Poached Egg, Polenta, Pancetta, Parmesan **186**

Roasted Chicken with Radicchio, Capers, Eggplant, and Crisp Bread **189**

Skillet Meatloaf with Tomato Glaze and Sweet Onion Slaw **190**

Steak Salad with Green Papaya **193**

Pork and Chile Chickpea Stew with or without Poached Eggs **194**

Pork Tacos with Cabbage Slaw **197**

Steamed Mussels with Sofrito **198**

Steamed Clams with Mushrooms, Coconut Milk, and Chiles **201**

Roasted Chicken Salad **202**

Roasted Chicken with Corn, Slow-Roasted Onions, and Tomato Salad **203**

Chicken and Dumplings **204**

Rib-Eye Steak with Salsa Verde, Escarole, and Pickled Chiles **207**

Seared Catfish with Chile-Tomato-Coconut Broth **208**

Pork Pozole **211**

Chicken Tortilla Chip Stew (Chilaquiles) **212**

Steak Salad with Pickled Radishes and Soy Vinaigrette **215**

Pot Roast with Celery Root Puree and Pomegranate-Parsley Salad **216**

SPAGHETTI WITH GARLIC AND OLIVE OIL
(SPAGHETTI AGLIO E OLIO)

SERVES 4

This is a simple oil-based sauce with a lot of garlic; it's so simple, and a classic Italian late-night meal. In your home, though, it can be infinitely flexible and made into a full meal with added bits of vegetables, leftover bites of protein, a fried or poached egg on top . . . and maybe a salad on the side. When the garlic is just getting golden brown, you will pull it off the heat to arrest the cooking a bit, and then add the pasta and some of the pasta water. Then put the pan back on the heat to bring it all together and finish with more olive oil and parsley. Serve with freshly grated Parmesan.

½ cup extra-virgin olive oil

5 garlic cloves, very thinly sliced

Pinch of crushed red pepper flakes

Kosher salt

1 pound spaghetti or other pasta

½ cup minced fresh flat-leaf parsley

½ cup freshly grated Parmesan cheese

In a large skillet, heat ¼ cup of the olive oil over medium heat. Add the garlic and gently cook until it is just getting golden, about 3 minutes. Add the pepper flakes and a pinch or two of salt. Remove from the heat in anticipation of the hot pasta being added to the pan.

Meanwhile, cook and drain the pasta as directed on page 51, reserving some of the pasta cooking water.

Return the skillet with the garlic and pepper flakes to medium heat. When it's hot again, add the drained pasta to the oil, along with ¼ cup pasta cooking water, and stir rapidly, until a creamy sauce forms and coats the noodles. Remove from the heat, add the remaining ¼ cup olive oil and the parsley, and stir well to combine. Top with the Parmesan and serve immediately.

GUSSY IT UP

This is one of those dishes that can serve as a template for lots of different meals. Just add a few things to the pasta as it's finishing in the skillet and boom: You have a different dinner. These ideas aren't strictly Italian, but they are delicious.

- spinach and feta cheese
- finely diced fresh tuna, added in at the last minute
- chopped Roasted Broccoli (see page 61)
- cooked white beans (see page 44) and tomatoes
- crumbled crisp bacon and anchovies
- Stir in a whipped egg right when you turn off the heat. Mix fast. You are heading into carbonara land.

ROASTED CHICKEN AND GRITS
WITH BROTH AND POACHED EGGS

SERVES 2

This is a very easy, homey dish for a cold night: a bowl of warm porridge surrounded by hot buttery broth and tender protein. Got some leftover roasted chicken? Great. Let's use it. If you don't, you can really use any leftover diced or pulled roasted meat or fish.

You know how to cook grits (page 77), so let's do that and finish with some creamy, 3-minute poached eggs.

Finally, you will have extra grits. Pour them into a buttered dish and chill in the fridge. Once hardened, you can cut them into squares and fry them in a little bit of butter or oil to crisp them up into grit cakes the next day for breakfast (or anytime).

1 cup regular or hominy grits

2½ cups milk

1 tablespoon Diamond Crystal kosher salt, or 2 teaspoons Morton kosher salt

½ cup grated Parmesan cheese

1 cup torn or shredded Roasted Chicken (page 68)

1 cup chicken stock

¼ cup minced scallions

1 tablespoon unsalted butter

4 large eggs

Freshly ground black pepper

8 HOURS TO 1 DAY AHEAD: In a 2-quart saucepan, combine the grits, milk, and 2½ cups water. Stir well, cover, and place in the fridge. Though I YELLED this instruction, it is optional. Just better.

DAY OF: Get the saucepan out of the fridge, place it over medium heat, and add the kosher salt. It will begin to cook very slowly, but stir often to get rid of any lumps and to make sure the grits don't stick to the bottom of the pot. When it comes to a boil, reduce the heat to a bare simmer. Cook for 1 hour, stirring a lot, and whisk in the Parmesan in the last few minutes. Keep warm. The grits should have the consistency of a fancy, smooth porridge.

In a small saucepan, combine the chicken, chicken stock, scallions, and butter. Bring to a boil over medium heat. Reduce the heat to low, cover, and heat through for 2 minutes.

Meanwhile, poach the eggs as directed on page 25.

To build your bowls: Grits first, about 1 cup per person, then divide the chicken and broth evenly between the two bowls. Then add the poached eggs to finish, with a pinch of salt and pepper on the eggs.

GUSSIED-UP INSTANT RAMEN

SERVES 1

Using leftover Roasted Chicken (page 68), let's make some instant ramen, the staple of undergrads across the land. This will add a few minutes to the 3 minutes it takes you to make that packet of ramen, but it will satisfy you ten times more. Of course, all the ingredients here are suggestions; mix and match or add or subtract as you like. I do recommend you add a little bit of leftover meat, the soft-boiled egg, and whatever vegetables you have lying around.

1 large egg ✳
Kosher salt
½ head baby bok choy, rinsed free of grit
1 tablespoon extra-virgin olive oil
1 small carrot
1 package instant ramen
¼ cup shredded Roasted Chicken (page 68)
Sesame seeds, for garnish
Cabbage kimchi, for serving

Fill a medium bowl with ice and enough water to submerge an egg. Gently place the egg in a small to medium pot and add liberally salted water to cover the egg by 2 inches. Set over high heat and bring the water to a boil. As soon as it comes to a boil, cover the pot, remove from the heat, and let sit for 6 minutes. Remove the egg from the pot and chill it in the ice bath for 5 minutes. Gently tap the bottom of the egg at the broad end to crack the shell. Using the side of your thumb, gently peel and discard the shell.

Cut the bok choy in half and season with a small pinch of salt. In a medium saucepan, heat the olive oil over medium-high heat. (This can be the saucepan you will make the ramen in.) When the oil begins to shimmer, place the bok choy in the pan, cut-side down, and sear for 2 to 3 minutes to char. Take it out of the pan and let cool, then chop.

Peel the carrot, then use the peeler to shave the carrot into ribbons. (Pro-tip / Hugh Hack: place the carrot ribbons in an ice bath; the cold water will curl the ribbons so you can make a nice "nest" with them.)

Now, I'm assuming all of you can read, so take out that wonderful ramen package and cook it according to the directions. Each brand will be a little different.

To serve, put the cooked noodles into your favorite bowl, then ladle the ramen broth on top. Slice your soft-boiled egg in half, and nestle on top of the noodles. Add the shaved carrots, the charred bok choy, and the chicken. Sprinkle with sesame seeds and serve with a nice spoonful of kimchi.

✳ Instead of soft-boiling the egg, you could poach it as directed on page 25.

SPAGHETTI AND MEATBALLS

SERVES 3 OR 4

Spaghetti and meatballs is a classic, but all too often the meatballs fall short of expectation. These ones are plump and juicy. If you have the tomato sauce done already from page 53, it is a pretty easy task.

1 cup torn up, crustless Italian bread

3 tablespoons buttermilk

½ medium onion, minced

2 garlic cloves, minced

1 ounce Parmigiano-Reggiano cheese, grated, plus more for serving

1 tablespoon chopped fresh flat-leaf parsley

1½ teaspoons Diamond Crystal kosher salt, or 1 teaspoon Morton kosher salt

½ teaspoon dried oregano

½ teaspoon ground fennel

½ teaspoon crushed red pepper flakes

Freshly ground black pepper

2 large egg yolks

½ pound ground beef (80% lean/ 20% fat)

½ pound ground pork

4 cups Back-Pocket Tomato Sauce (page 53)

1 pound spaghetti

Fresh basil leaves, hand-torn

In a bowl, combine the bread and buttermilk (I use a fork to press the bread to ensure all the bread is moistened with the buttermilk). Let this mixture hang for about 10 minutes. Add the onion, garlic, Parmigiano, parsley, salt, oregano, fennel, pepper flakes, black pepper to taste, and the egg yolks and mix until homogenous.

In a separate bowl, mix together the ground beef and ground pork with your hands until the meat mixture feels tacky. Combine the two mixtures and mix together evenly. Ideally, allow the mixture to chill in the refrigerator for at least 1 hour; this helps keep the meatballs tender and moist. Portion the mixture into 8 balls and place evenly spaced on a sheet pan.

Arrange an oven rack in the highest position and preheat the broiler.

Broil the meatballs until browned on top, about 4 minutes. Flip and broil for another 4 minutes.

Meanwhile, in a medium saucepan, bring the tomato sauce to a simmer.

Remove the browned meatballs from the oven and gently place them in the simmering sauce (just the meatballs, not the juices that leaked from them onto the sheet pan). Let the meatballs simmer, turning them occasionally, until cooked through, about 10 minutes. They should be just hot in the center.

Meanwhile, cook the spaghetti as directed on page 51.

Serve the meatballs and sauce over the spaghetti and garnish with torn basil and grated Parmigiano.

LOUISIANA-STYLE DIRTY RICE
WITH GREENS

**SERVES 2 OR 3
AS A MAIN COURSE,
4 TO 6 AS
A SIDE DISH**

This is a flavor-packed ode to Louisiana, which is home to some of America's greatest rice dishes. It's a sautéed rice (somewhere between risotto and fried rice) that uses cold leftover cooked rice that is made tasty with onion and spices. The key is the chicken livers, which, before you flip the page, ARE AMAZING in this rice. For ten years I fed my kids dirty rice (albeit with less cayenne), and they never knew it had livers in it. They just knew it was great. The livers cook into something like a subtle ground meat filling, giving it a deep flavor.

FOR THE SPICE MIX

1 teaspoon Diamond Crystal kosher salt, or ½ teaspoon Morton kosher salt

1 teaspoon smoked paprika

½ teaspoon mustard powder

½ teaspoon ground cumin

Pinch of cayenne pepper

Freshly ground black pepper to taste

FOR THE RICE

2 tablespoons canola oil

½ cup minced yellow onion

¼ cup minced celery

¼ cup minced poblano pepper

3 garlic cloves, minced

½ cup chicken livers, finely chopped

4 cups Foolproof Rice (page 41), cold or at room temperature

1 cup chicken stock

3 cups chopped turnip greens or other hearty greens

4 large eggs (optional), for serving

Make the spice mix: In a bowl, combine the salt, smoked paprika, mustard, cumin, cayenne, and pepper. (It's a great spice mix; you can make it in bigger batches, and have it ready for this rice or for seasoning meats.)

Make the rice: In a large skillet, heat the oil over medium-high heat until shimmering-hot. Add the onion, celery, and poblano and cook for 2 minutes, stirring a couple of times. Add the garlic, chicken livers, and spice mix and stir well. Add the rice, stock, and turnip greens and stir well to combine. Cook until the rice is hot all the way through and the greens are tender, about 5 minutes.

If desired, poach the eggs as directed on page 25.

Serve, topped with poached eggs, if you want.

PASTA WITH TOMATO AND CURED PORK

(BUCATINI AMATRICIANA)

<u>SERVES 4</u>

Bucatini is a pasta, long like spaghetti but hollow inside, but you can use any long shape, like spaghetti or linguine for this. Amatriciana is one of the classic pasta sauces of Rome, even though it comes from a town a couple hours away, called Amatrice. It's based on the flavor match of tomato and guanciale, a beautifully fatty and flavorful cured pork jowl. If you can't get it, you can try pancetta (Italian cured pork belly) or, in a pinch, bacon.

Kosher salt

1 tablespoon olive oil

¼ pound finely diced guanciale, pancetta, or bacon

½ cup sliced (¼ inch thick) red onion

1 garlic clove, minced

1 tablespoon fresh marjoram or oregano leaves

¼ teaspoon crushed red pepper flakes

2 cups Back-Pocket Tomato Sauce (page 53)

1 pound bucatini pasta

½ cup torn fresh basil leaves

1 tablespoon unsalted butter

2 tablespoons grated Pecorino Romano cheese, plus more for serving

Set a large pot of water over high heat to bring to a boil, salting it as directed on page 51.

Set a large skillet over medium-high heat. When warm, add the olive oil and guanciale. Cook until the fat has rendered out and the meat is starting to crisp, about 4 minutes. Add the onions, spread them out, and cook until they have a good amount of color on one side, about 5 minutes. Add the garlic, marjoram, and pepper flakes and cook for a minute. Add the tomato sauce, bring to a simmer, then reduce the heat to let it simmer, not boil, for 15 minutes to reduce the sauce a bit. Taste and season with salt until the flavors pop. Turn the heat to very low to mellow out while you cook the pasta.

Add the pasta to the boiling water and cook as directed on page 51, scooping out a coffee cup full of water from the pasta pot before draining. Add the pasta right away to the pan with the sauce. Stir and toss it well with the sauce and stir in the basil, butter, and Pecorino, adding some pasta water if it is looking like it needs a touch of liquid to come together. Toss well and portion into bowls. Serve with more cheese on top, if desired.

CRISPED RICE
WITH SAUSAGE AND KIMCHI

SERVES 2

This is a meal that requires a couple of pans, but it is worth it. It is a textural delight that punches with acid and heat, and comforts with meaty sausage and the pillow of a poached egg. If you're not already familiar with cabbage kimchi, you are in for a treat. A Korean pickled cabbage, it sings with chile, acidity, and a delicious funk. If you are still acquiring the taste for it, you can use less. (You can also sauté it in a little butter, which mellows it out a bit.)

The trick to this dish is the rice, which uses a Thai technique, where the already cooked rice is oiled prior to crisping in a hot pan. Works like a charm.

No breakfast sausage? Use some cooked chicken, tofu, shrimp, or whatever is hanging out in your fridge.

2 tablespoons peanut or canola oil, plus more if needed

¼ pound bulk breakfast sausage

2 cups Foolproof Rice (page 41), cooled and chilled

Kosher salt

½ cup chopped napa cabbage kimchi

2 tablespoons fresh cilantro leaves

1 tablespoon minced scallions

1 tablespoon freshly squeezed lime juice

2 tablespoons roasted unsalted peanuts, lightly crushed

2 large eggs (optional), at room temperature

Set a large skillet over medium-high heat. Add 1 tablespoon of the oil and then break up the sausage into the pan. Cook until cooked through, about 6 minutes, stirring every minute or so. Remove to a bowl.

Clean out the sausage pan and return it to medium-high heat ✱. While it is heating up, place the cold cooked rice in a bowl, crumble it with your hands, and add the remaining 1 tablespoon peanut oil. Mix well with your hands to get some of the oil on every kernel of rice. If it seems like not enough oil, drizzle in a little more. When the pan is nice and hot, place the rice in the pan and press down a little bit with a spatula to lay down an even foundation of rice. Don't mess with it for about 5 minutes, and then lift a corner of it to see how the crisping is coming along.

Begin to break it up a little bit when it is nicely crisped and golden. Remove from the heat. Crumble the cooked sausage into the rice and season to taste with a pinch of salt.

In a medium bowl, combine the kimchi, cilantro, scallions, lime juice, and peanuts. Toss gently to combine.

If using, poach the eggs as directed on page 25.

Divide the crisp rice and sausage between two bowls. Add a hot poached egg to each and then evenly divide the kimchi salad over the top of the eggs.

✱ If you want to double this recipe, either use a really big pan (12 inches) for the rice or do this in batches, to avoid undercrisping the rice.

SPAGHETTI WITH SHRIMP AND LEEKS

SERVES 4

This is a 20-minute meal that is straight-up tasty, with one qualifier: You have to find good shrimp. You will start cooking the shrimp halfway through the leek cooking time, but I spell that out below.

Kosher salt

2 large leeks

2 tablespoons unsalted butter

1 pound spaghetti

½ cup chicken stock

½ cup crème fraîche, sour cream, or heavy cream

Big pinch of crushed red pepper flakes

½ teaspoon grated lemon zest (grate the lemon right on a grater/zester to get just the yellow zest)

1 pound large domestic white shrimp, peeled, tails off, and deveined

Freshly ground black pepper

Set a large pot of water over high heat to bring to a boil for the pasta, salting it as directed on page 51.

Trim off the dark green tops of the leeks, saving them for stock, leaving the white and pale green parts. Halve the leeks lengthwise and rinse between the leaves to dislodge any dirt or sand trapped between them. Cut the leeks crosswise in half-moon slices about ¼ inch thick.

In a large skillet, heat the butter over medium heat until it melts, bubbles, and froths. Add the leeks and cook for 10 minutes, stirring every minute or so, until very soft.

Meanwhile, add the spaghetti to the boiling water and start cooking as directed on page 51.

Back to the leeks. Once the leeks have softened, add the stock, crème fraîche, pepper flakes, and lemon zest and mix well. Season to taste with salt. Cook for another 3 minutes to meld the flavors.

Place the shrimp on a plate, spread out, and season them with a few pinches of salt. Add the shrimp to the leek sauce and cook, stirring occasionally, just until they all turn pink on both sides (which means they are pretty much cooked through), about 3 minutes. Remove from the heat if you need to wait for the pasta to finish cooking.

Scoop out ½ cup of the pasta water with a coffee cup. Drain the pasta in a colander. Transfer the pasta to the skillet with the shrimp if it will fit, or return it to its cooking pot and add the leek/shrimp mixture to it. Toss it all together with tongs over medium-high heat, adding a splash of pasta water to unify everything and moisten the pasta if need be. Season with pepper. Plate it up and serve.

WHEAT BERRY SALAD
WITH TOMATO, FETA, MINT, AND OLIVES

SERVES 4

Wheat berries are the whole kernel of wheat. If ground, they become w ...e wheat flour. They cook like rice (see Foolproof Rice, page 41) and they have a nutty flavor and chewiness that I love. If the phrase "whole wheat" makes you think of dry, flavorless "health food," I think you just haven't had good whole wheat yet. This fresh salad is one way to do it, with a ton of textures and flavors.

Use tomatoes that have taste. Look for ones that smell good, don't feel totally hard, and are free of blemishes and soft spots. Ideally you would get some local heirlooms, but I have no problem with hothouse tomatoes.

Feta is a fresh brined cheese. I particularly like sheep's milk feta from France, but there are lots of good ones. Your forefinger and thumb can crumble feta in no time at all, so don't buy it precrumbled.

Sumac is an acidic spice that is almost lemony in flavor. It is at home in Middle Eastern food, but that influence spreads to the Mediterranean flavors that this salad evokes. It is sold ground, and can be found in many grocery stores.

Kosher salt
½ cup wheat berries ✱
4 medium tomatoes, diced
½ cup minced scallions
½ cup torn fresh mint leaves
½ cup pitted Kalamata olives
½ cup Classic Vinaigrette (page 27)
1 teaspoon ground sumac
½ cup crumbled feta cheese
Freshly ground black pepper

In a large pot, bring 2 quarts water to a boil over high heat. Salt it until it tastes salty, but not gross.

Rinse the wheat berries in a bowl, under cold running water. Drain and add them to the water when it's at a rolling boil. Cook about 20 minutes. Some wheat berries can take longer, so just taste them along the way. You are looking for them to be tender with a touch of chewiness. Drain and spread the wheat berries out on a platter or sheet pan to cool quickly.

In a salad bowl, combine the wheat berries, tomatoes, scallions, mint, and olives. In a small bowl, whisk the vinaigrette with the sumac. Dress the vegetables with

about half of it. Season with a pinch of salt, then add the feta and some pepper. Taste and add more salt or dressing, toss gently again, and serve. Because this salad doesn't have lettuces and leafy greens in it, it will keep in the fridge for 5 days. Perfect for lunch at work in a pinch.

✱ If you want, you can cook double the amount of wheat berries, then use half of them for the salad and the other half for something else later. It doesn't take any more time or effort to cook more. Store them in a sealed storage container in the fridge, and then use them in salads, soups, or heated up with a little stock and butter as a side to most anything.

AVATELLI
WITH CHICKPEAS, TOMATO SAUCE, RICOTTA, AND BASIL

SERVES 4

These are simple flavors that work together. The chickpeas give you a nuttiness and protein, the ricotta a creaminess, and it all serves as a reminder that pasta with tomato sauce is a perfect dish, and a perfect base to riff off of and add to. Cavatelli are small shells that kind of look like tiny sandwich buns, and the sauce has a chance to cling well to the pasta. If you can't find cavatelli, orecchiette or penne would be great substitutes, but really you can use anything in the dried pasta arena.

1 pound cavatelli or other dried pasta

1 tablespoon olive oil

½ cup minced yellow onion

2 garlic cloves, thinly sliced

2 cups cooked chickpeas, homemade (page 44), or 1 (15-ounce) can, rinsed and drained

2 cups Back-Pocket Tomato Sauce (page 53)

Kosher salt

½ cup fresh ricotta cheese

1 cup torn fresh basil leaves

Cook the pasta as directed on page 51. Cavatelli will take a bit longer than spaghetti, so just check it as it cooks.

Meanwhile, in a large skillet, heat the olive oil over medium-high heat until hot. Add the onion and garlic and cook, stirring, for 2 minutes. Add the chickpeas and tomato sauce, bring to a simmer, and season to taste with some salt (it may need just a pinch, because the tomato sauce is already seasoned). When the pasta is just finishing up, add the ricotta and basil leaves to the tomato sauce.

Scoop out a cup of the pasta water, then drain the pasta and add it to the sauce. Add a touch of pasta water to the skillet and toss well to combine the pasta with the sauce.

SAVANNAH RED RICE

**SERVES 1 TO 3
AS A MAIN COURSE,
4 AS A SIDE DISH**

This regional Southern recipe is a winner, often thought of as the signature dish of coastal Georgia. It's red from tomato—here we'll use some sofrito from page 67—and gets a lot of smoky, rich flavor from bacon. Because I want to encourage you to have cooked rice on hand in your fridge (like for fried rice on page 114), this recipe will call for that, but if you want to cook rice fresh just for this, please go ahead. This is a 10-minute delight so you have no excuses.

½ pound bacon, cut into ½-inch pieces

2 tablespoons unsalted butter

¼ cup minced celery

½ cup Red Sofrito (page 67)

½ teaspoon cayenne pepper

½ cup chicken stock

2 cups Foolproof Rice (page 41)

A few spoonfuls sour cream, for garnish

A few pinches of sliced scallions, for garnish

Freshly ground black pepper

Hot sauce, for serving

Heat a large sauté pan over medium-low heat. Add the bacon, spread it out, and cook until a good amount of the fat has rendered out, about 8 minutes. Add the butter and celery and increase the heat to medium. Cook the celery until starting to soften, about 2 minutes. Add the sofrito and cayenne and cook for 4 minutes to bring it together.

Add the chicken stock and bring to a boil. Stir the cooked rice into the sofrito base until it's evenly distributed. Keep cooking until the liquid is absorbed by the rice and the mixture has some crunchy bites on the bottom. Scoop into a bowl, garnish with sour cream and scallions, season with pepper, and serve hot sauce on the side.

POLENTA
WITH PORK, APPLES, AND SLOW-ROASTED ONION

SERVES 2

If you have leftover pork from page 48, then buy an apple, make some p
and you have a really hearty dinner. This is a fall fave.

½ recipe Soft Polenta (page 77)

1 tablespoon canola oil

½ pound Slow-Roasted Pork Shoulder
(page 48), shredded

1 crisp red apple, sliced into wedges

1 cup Slow-Roasted Onion quarters
(page 59)

½ cup apple cider

2 tablespoons minced fresh flat-leaf
parsley

Kosher salt

1 tablespoon extra-virgin olive oil

Cook the polenta as directed, and when it's done, keep it warm until ready to plate. (Or, if you're using it cold from the fridge, you can reheat it with a splash of water in a microwave or a saucepan over medium-low heat, stirring to re-soften it.)

Set a large skillet over medium heat. Add the canola oil and place the pork in one half of the pan and the apple wedges in the other. Cook for about 4 minutes,

and then turn the apples over and cook for another 2 minutes. The pork will be getting crisp, and that's good. Add the onions and cider to the pan and allow it to cook down for 1 minute. Add the parsley. Season it all with a pinch or two of salt.

Divide the polenta between two bowls. Scatter the pork and apples over the polenta, drizzle with the olive oil, and serve.

SPAGHETTI WITH BASIL PESTO

SERVES 4

Such a simple mix of ingredients results in an iconic dish. There are many methods for making pesto, and it's something you can riff on infinitely. Just be sure to use a nice amount of soft herb (basil is classic, obviously), good olive oil, a touch of garlic, salty hard cheese, and toasted nuts. Pine nuts are the traditional choice, but they can be expensive. If almonds or walnuts or even peanuts are more available to you, don't hesitate to use them. We're just making dinner here, people.

Once you have made the pesto, cook a pound of pasta and mix them together in a large bowl. Add a touch of the pasta cooking water to bring it all together.

You can also make the pesto and freeze it (in ice cube trays is great; just pop out the cubes once frozen and put them in a freezer bag so you can have them on hand for a quick meal). I do suggest skipping the cheese if you're going to freeze the pesto, though, and just adding it when you thaw the pesto and use it. Cheese doesn't like the freezer.

1 teaspoon Diamond Crystal kosher salt, or ½ teaspoon Morton kosher salt

3 cups lightly packed fresh basil leaves

3 garlic cloves, minced

¼ cup pine nuts or other nuts, toasted

⅔ cup extra-virgin olive oil

⅔ cup grated Pecorino Romano or other salty hard cheese, like Parmesan

Freshly ground black pepper

1 pound spaghetti

Set a large pot of water over high heat to bring to a boil, salting it as directed on page 51.

In a food processor or blender, combine the basil, ¼ cup cold water, garlic, and pine nuts. With the machine running, slowly drizzle in the oil to emulsify. Blend until it's smooth. Turn off the motor. Add the cheese and pulse a couple of times to incorporate. Season with the salt and pepper to taste and pulse a couple of times to mix in. Transfer to a large bowl.

Add the pasta to the pot of water and cook as directed on page 51, scooping out a coffee cup full of water from the pasta pot before draining. Add the pasta to the bowl of pesto. Toss it with tongs and add a small splash of the pasta cooking water to moisten the pasta. Serve.

FRIED RICE
WITH PORK AND KIMCHI

<u>SERVES 2</u>

Fried rice is the natural habitat for that cold cooked rice that has been sitting in your fridge for a couple of days. It is a fast and easy meal that is better than most you can get delivered to your door. And you control the ingredients. Pea shoots? Radishes? Iceberg lettuce? Anything goes. Use up those leftovers and create a dish that everyone loves. This particular version is chock-full of vegetables, uses leftover roast pork from page 48, and features the spicy, tart, deep flavor of kimchi, which I love. What's key is the technique. You can swap in and out vegetables, proteins, and seasonings as you wish, and once you know how to make fried rice—get the pan really hot, use ingredients precooked or cut up small (so they'll cook faster), and just keep tasting and adding seasoning until it's delicious—you can make a meal whenever you have rice lying around.

2 large eggs

Kosher salt

Canola oil

1 cup shredded Slow-Roasted Pork Shoulder (page 48)

1 tablespoon minced fresh ginger

1 shallot, minced

½ cup small-diced carrot

½ cup frozen peas, thawed

2 cups Foolproof Rice (page 41)

½ cup chopped kimchi

¼ cup sliced scallions

1 tablespoon soy sauce

1 tablespoon sesame oil

In a small bowl, whisk the eggs with a pinch of salt.

Set a large skillet over high heat and heat it for a few minutes, until piping hot, and add a good splash of the canola oil, enough to coat the pan. When you see a wisp of smoke from the oil, add the eggs, let them set for 30 seconds, flip them and break them up with a spatula, then remove the cooked egg to a bowl. Set aside. If your pan was hot enough and you used enough oil, the egg shouldn't stick. But if you have some stuck bits of egg, wipe out the pan or rinse it out and dry it.

Set the pan back over high heat and add 1 tablespoon canola oil. When the oil is hot, add the pork, ginger, and shallot, spread it all out, and let it crisp for 1 minute. Add the carrot, peas, and rice. Stir it together and press it down. You may need to add another splash of oil if it's looking dry. Cook until the rice is slightly crisped and warm through, about 4 minutes.

Add the cooked egg, kimchi, scallions, soy sauce, and sesame oil. Mix well and heat through, about 1 minute. Serve.

CHEF'S SALAD

SERVES 4

The chef's salad was surely created by a cook tasked with cleaning out the fridge, but it's a great combination of ingredients that meld together to give crunch and balance. And you can mix and match: No ham? Use some cooked chicken. No boiled egg? Add some tofu. No carrots? No biggie. I would miss that crunch, but I'll also show you how to make some pan-fried croutons. (It's kind of like cooking grilled cheese, only the bread is in pieces and there is no cheese.)

When would I eat this? About once a week for dinner. If you know you are going to be busy, get the cutting done in your downtime, up to 24 hours in advance, and then assemble and dress it when you are ready for a meal.

2 cups chopped iceberg lettuce

1 head butter lettuce, torn into large bite-size pieces

2 medium tomatoes, cored and diced

1 cup sliced carrot rounds, about ¼ inch thick

1 cup diced cucumber

1 cup diced celery

½ cup thinly sliced red onion

Pan-Fried Croutons (recipe follows)

½ cup Classic Vinaigrette (page 27), or other dressing

Kosher salt

1 cup diced aged cheddar cheese

¼ pound sliced Black Forest ham, chopped

1 avocado

1 tablespoon freshly squeezed lime juice

4 large eggs, hard-boiled and quartered

Freshly ground black pepper

In a large bowl (or a big pot if you don't have a big bowl), mix together the iceberg, butter lettuce, tomatoes, carrots, cucumber, celery, onion, and croutons. Add ¼ cup of the vinaigrette to dress the salad. Season with a pinch or two of salt and toss gently. Add the cheddar and ham, toss again, adding more of the vinaigrette if you want.

Pit and dice the avocado ✱. Season the avocado with a touch of salt and the lime juice.

Divide the salad onto four plates. Divide the avocado evenly over the salads, and then the boiled eggs. Drizzle a little of the vinaigrette onto them and then grind some fresh pepper on top.

✱ Cut the avocado around the pit and get the pit out. Using your knife, cut a checkerboard pattern into the avocado, all the way to the skin, then scoop all the flesh out with a spoon—boom, diced avocado.

PAN-FRIED CROUTONS

MAKES 2 CUPS

⅓ cup olive oil

2 cups cubed or torn bread (about ½-inch cube-like shapes)

Kosher salt

Set a large skillet over medium heat. Add the olive oil and wait for it to get shimmering-hot. Add the bread, move it around so the pieces aren't crowded, and just keep an eye on things. They will begin to brown after about 2 minutes. Turn them with a spoon.

Season with a couple of pinches of salt. Continue cooking until they are all toasty and golden, about 5 minutes total. Scoop the croutons to a plate lined with paper towels to wick away any excess oil.

POACHED EGG AND BACON SALAD

Frisée, escarole, Belgian endive, radicchio, puntarelle, and even daisies are all from the endive family, and they enliven so much. They are beautifully bitter but refreshing. This salad takes those greens and matches them with a poached egg, smoky bacon, and vinaigrette. It's a meal of a salad, served with a hunk of bread. And it really takes no time at all.

For this we will use our core vinaigrette recipe, but we will add some lemon juice to it. The extra acid will cut the richness of the egg and bacon and balance out the salad.

½ pound bacon, cut into ½-inch pieces

1 Belgian endive, sliced

2 cups chopped escarole or other hearty greens

¼ cup chopped fresh flat-leaf parsley

1 tablespoon freshly squeezed lemon juice

¼ cup Classic Vinaigrette (page 27)

Kosher salt and freshly ground black pepper

2 large eggs

Place a large skillet on the stove. Add the bacon to the cold pan and turn the burner to medium. Slowly cook the bacon until crisp, stirring every few minutes, about 10 minutes total. Remove the bacon from the pan with a slotted spoon and spread it out on a plate lined with paper towels to drain. (Cool the rendered bacon fat and save it for another time. It's great for sautéing potatoes or adding bacon flavor to things. You can also stir the bacon fat into the vinaigrette, but you'll want to up the acid with more lemon.)

In a large bowl, combine the Belgian endive, escarole, and parsley. Add the bacon and toss well to mix. Add the lemon juice to the vinaigrette, stir to combine, then dress the greens and bacon with the vinaigrette to taste—start with a couple tablespoons, taste, and add more if you want. Season with salt to taste, toss again, and set aside.

Poach the eggs as directed on page 25.

Divide the salad onto two plates and then nestle a poached egg on each. Sprinkle a little salt and pepper on each egg.

AVOCADO TOAST
WITH FETA AND ROASTED BROCCOLI

SERVES 2

I know you have spent $9 on toast. I see the sales. But now you can make a delicious, full-meal version of avocado toast, resplendent with broccoli, feta, and radishes, grounded with smoky paprika butter. You got this. (And you can really use whatever other kind of cheese or vegetable you want.)

2 tablespoons unsalted butter,
  at room temperature

1 teaspoon smoked paprika

1 lime, halved

Kosher salt

1 avocado

2 slices whole-grain bread

½ recipe Roasted Broccoli (page 61)
  or other roasted veg

2 tablespoons crumbled feta cheese,
  or other cheese like sharp cheddar

2 radishes or other crisp vegetable,
  thinly sliced

First, let's make a very simple smoked paprika butter. In a small bowl, combine the soft butter and smoked paprika. Squeeze in a smidge of lime juice and season with a pinch of salt. Mix well with a fork.

Pit and dice the avocado (see ✳, page 117) into a small bowl. Squeeze some lime juice onto the avocado (this will stave off browning). Season the avocado with a nice pinch of salt and mash it up with a fork.

Toast the bread and while it's still hot, slather it evenly with smoked paprika butter to taste. Evenly spread the avocado over the toasts and then arrange some roasted broccoli on each, crumble some feta over the top, and dot with radish slices. Finish with a tiny squeeze of lime.

GRILLED CHEESE
WITH PEAR AND SLOW-COOKED ONIONS

SERVES 1

This is a classic example of how to turn something simple into something more. A grilled cheese with the sweet-savory combo of pears and meltingly soft roasted onions from page 59 is just delicious—like a cheese plate in sandwich form. Pair with a salad and you have a meal. You have your choice of cheese in this, but I would go Gruyère. It is a good melting cheese and has a ton of flavor. Use a bread that tastes great and has some structure. The bakery a couple of blocks away from me has a great whole wheat French loaf that is rustic and wonderful; try this with something you'd describe that way.

1 tablespoon unsalted butter, at room temperature

2 slices good-quality bread

3 ounces sliced Gruyère cheese

½ pear, cored and thinly sliced

1 quarter Slow-Roasted Onions (page 59)

Pinch of kosher salt

Butter one side of each of the bread slices. Set a large skillet over medium or medium-low heat and when it is hot, place the bread butter-side down in the pan. Evenly divide the cheese between the slices of bread. Toast the bread to golden brown, 3 to 5 minutes, depending on your stove and pan, occasionally peeking to see how the toasting is progressing.

The cheese will begin to melt, and once the bread is golden, pile the pear and onions onto one side. Season the onions with the salt. Put the other side of the sandwich on top of it. Reduce the heat to low and cook 1 more minute on one side and then 1 minute on the other, to let the cheese fully melt. Eat.

CHICKEN AND POTATO SALAD
WITH WHITE WINE AND HERBS

SERVES 4

You love chicken. You love little creamy potatoes. You love copious amounts of fresh herbs. Let's get this together and make it right, tossed with a little white wine and vinaigrette. (If you avoid alcohol, bring the wine to a boil in a small pan to evaporate the alcohol and let it cool.) This relies on you having some roasted chicken around, so it can be leftovers or you can roast one just for this purpose, and use the rest in another chicken-based recipe.

Incidentally, once you've completed the first paragraph of this recipe, congratulations, you just made boiled potatoes. You can come back to this, make them and dress them with butter, sour cream, and chives for a great side dish, or lightly crush them and top with olive oil and grated lemon zest and put them next to a piece of fish, or, or, or . . .

1 pound small red potatoes (also called "new" or "creamer"), about the size of a Ping-Pong ball

Kosher salt

4 cups pulled Roasted Chicken (page 68)

¼ cup dry white wine

¾ cup Classic Vinaigrette (page 27)

2 tablespoons chopped fresh flat-leaf parsley

1 tablespoon chopped fresh thyme leaves

1 tablespoon chopped fresh tarragon leaves

¼ cup minced scallions

Freshly ground black pepper

Place the potatoes in a pot and cover with cold water by 1 inch. Bring to a boil over medium-high heat and add 1 tablespoon salt. Reduce the heat to medium-low and simmer until tender, about 15 minutes. (They may cook faster or slower, so check at about 12 minutes. They are done when a sharp, pointy knife slides into them with little resistance.) Drain the potatoes. When they are cool enough to handle, slice them. You want them bite-size. When you are slicing cooked potatoes, it helps to wipe down the knife after every slice to make clean cuts.

In a large bowl, combine the potatoes (still warm is best; it helps them absorb dressing), the chicken, white wine, vinaigrette, parsley, thyme, tarragon, and scallions. Season with salt to taste and add a good number of grinds of pepper. Toss well to get everything together.

FENNEL AND WHITE BEAN SALAD

**SERVES 4 AS
A SIDE DISH**

Fennel and white beans are a natural match; the crunch of fresh fennel and its slightly licorice-y flavor are great contrasts to creamy, earthy beans. Add some shallots and dill and you have the easiest side to accomplish, yet one that will impress. It's a great, healthful accompaniment to a roasted pork chop, chicken, or steak—both refreshing and satisfying.

This recipe uses the core vinaigrette on page 27 and the technique for cooking beans from page 44, but I am not in your kitchen, and should you use canned beans, I will never find out. (And in any case, I would smile and nod.) Do what you want. There is no shame in canned bean land.

1 fennel bulb, baseball size, stalks
  and fronds removed

1 shallot, thinly sliced into rounds

¼ cup chopped fresh dill

Kosher salt

1 tablespoon freshly squeezed lemon
  juice

2 tablespoons extra-virgin olive oil

Pinch of crushed red pepper flakes

1½ cups cooked white beans,
  homemade (page 44) or canned
  (rinsed and drained)

¼ cup Classic Vinaigrette (page 27)

Slice the fennel bulb in half, from top to bottom. Cut out the thick core with your knife. Then slice the fennel thinly against the grain to make half-moon slices. Place in a bowl and add the shallot, dill, a pinch or two of salt, the lemon juice, olive oil, and pepper flakes. Toss well. The flavor and texture will improve if you let it sit at room temperature for a while, ideally 1 hour.

Add the drained beans and the vinaigrette. Mix well, taste, and season with salt until the flavors pop. Beans are notorious for needing salt, so make sure you taste it well.

CUBAN GRILLED CHEESE

SERVES 1 PRETTY HUNGRY PERSON

This is a marrying of the splendid flavors of a Cuban sandwich with the methodology of a grilled cheese (which you know from page 57). It uses some leftovers from the slow-roasted pork shoulder from page 48, regular sliced ham, the neon beauty of yellow mustard, Swiss cheese, and some plain Jane dill pickles to melt into a meal you will crave.

1 tablespoon canola oil

¾ cup shredded Slow-Roasted Pork Shoulder (page 48)

2 tablespoons unsalted butter, at room temperature

2 large slices bread (preferably sourdough), ½ inch thick

3 ounces sliced Swiss cheese

3 ounces thinly sliced deli ham

1 large dill pickle, thinly sliced lengthwise

1 tablespoon yellow mustard

Kosher salt

Set a small skillet over medium heat. Add the canola oil and when the oil is hot, add the shredded pork. Crisp this up for a few minutes, turning it once in a while, as you assemble the sandwich.

Generously butter *one side* of each of the bread slices. (You don't have to use all the butter if you don't want to; it's just quicker for it to come to spreadable consistency if you cut off a couple tablespoons rather than wait for the whole stick to warm up.)

Set a large skillet over medium or medium-low heat and when it is hot, place the bread, butter-side down, in the pan. Evenly divide the Swiss cheese between the slices of bread. Toast the bread to golden brown, 3 to 5 minutes, depending on your stove and pan, occasionally peeking to see how the toasting is progressing. Once the cheese melts, add the ham and pickles to one half of the sandwich. Liberally smear the mustard on the pickles and then pile on the crisp pork shoulder. Take the other cheese bread and make it into a sandwich, pressing down to compress all of it. Reduce the heat to low and cook 1 more minute on each side, to let the cheese fully melt. Eat.

ICEBERG SALAD
WITH CELERY, PINE NUTS, AND CHEESE

SERVES 4 TO 6

This is a home version of a fancy restaurant salad that has all sorts of pale endives, a zingy vinaigrette, and a good amount of shaved Parmesan cheese. This version is a thrifty rendition, harnessing the beauty that is the ubiquitous iceberg lettuce. Crisp and constant is the way with the iceberg. Celery, also underrated, also thrifty, is wonderful. Don't @ me. Peel it first, though. Yes, peel it, with a peeler. It takes a couple seconds, and you will get rid of its strings and people will marvel at this amazing, delicate celery they have only ever had at your house.

Pine nuts are expensive and often past their prime, by which I mean they have gone rancid. Buy them from a store that moves a lot of them, use them within a couple of months, and if they taste off then they probably are.

Cotija is the cheese you get on Mexican street corn. It is a hard cheese that is usually found already grated; it's salty and delicious. It, too, is thrifty. This is a thrifty dish all over the place. If you prefer Parmesan, go ahead and use that, or any other hard, grateable cheese.

1 tablespoon extra-virgin olive oil

½ cup pine nuts

3 or 4 stalks celery

1 head iceberg lettuce, cored and chopped into bite-size pieces

¼ to ½ cup Classic Vinaigrette (page 27)

Kosher salt

Plenty of grated Cotija cheese

In a medium skillet, heat the olive oil over medium heat until shimmering-hot. Add the pine nuts and toast, stirring, for 2 minutes. Transfer to a paper towel to wick some of the oil off of the nuts. When the nuts are cool, place them on a cutting board and coarsely chop them a couple of times. We don't want them powdered, just broken down a bit.

Using a vegetable peeler, peel the outside curve of the celery; you'll see the strings in the layer you're peeling off. You don't have to go crazy; just getting rid of that first layer or two is fine. Thinly slice the celery stalks to get 2 cups of slices. Snack on the rest.

Put the lettuce, celery, and nuts in a large bowl. Add vinaigrette to taste and season with some salt. Toss well and then shower with the Cotija cheese.

LUXE PATTY MELT WITH SLOW-ROASTED ONIONS AND PICKLES

**MAKES 4
PATTY MELTS**

Let's use the burgers from page 36, but finish them in the style of a patty melt, kind of a cross between a burger and a grilled cheese. We'll melt the cheese under the broiler, which is that underused oven function that produces high heat to melt, crisp, or char the top of your food.

OH, AND THERE IS A SPECIAL SAUCE. Which is a wonderful thing to put on just about any sandwich. Let's do it.

8 slices rye bread, toasted

Burgers (page 36), cooked but not assembled into sandwiches

8 slices medium cheddar cheese

1 cup Slow-Roasted Onions (page 59)

½ cup Special Sauce (recipe follows)

½ cup minced dill pickle

Preheat the oven broiler to high.

Arrange 4 slices of the toast on a sheet pan and top each with a cooked burger patty. Top each with 2 slices cheese, covering the burger. Place under the broiler to melt, watching them closely.

Remove the pan from the oven (it's hot!), top each sandwich with roasted onions, a dollop of special sauce, and a good mound of chopped pickle. Top with the other slices of toast. Cut each sandwich in half and serve.

SPECIAL SAUCE

MAKES ABOUT ¾ CUP

1 tablespoon Dijon mustard

½ cup mayonnaise

2 tablespoons ketchup

1 shallot, minced

1 tablespoon minced fresh dill

1 teaspoon smoked paprika

1 tablespoon freshly squeezed lemon juice

½ teaspoon Diamond Crystal kosher salt, or ¼ teaspoon Morton kosher salt

In a bowl, stir everything together well. The sauce will keep refrigerated for a week or so.

RED CHECK SALAD

SERVES 4 TO 6

This salad is what you would expect to get at the best Italian-American restaurant. You know, the old-school one that looks like it was already old in 1961 and hasn't changed a bit since. The menu always has chicken Milanese, and the pastas are simple classics. But the salad is what always gets me. It is just so zesty and fun.

We'll use the 3:1 oil-to-acid ratio and technique we learned in the vinaigrette building block on page 27, but we are going to change the ingredients up a bit for a different flavor.

FOR THE RED CHECK
VINAIGRETTE

½ cup extra-virgin olive oil

3 tablespoons red wine vinegar

1 tablespoon mayonnaise

1 teaspoon dried oregano

1 garlic clove, minced

½ teaspoon Diamond Crystal
kosher salt, or ¼ teaspoon
Morton kosher salt

Freshly ground black pepper

FOR THE SALAD

1 head iceberg lettuce, cored and
chopped

2 medium heirloom tomatoes when
in season, 4 ripe plum tomatoes
when not

½ teaspoon Diamond Crystal
kosher salt, or ¼ teaspoon
Morton kosher salt

¼ cup fresh flat-leaf parsley leaves

½ cup sliced pepperoncini peppers

Plenty of grated Parmesan cheese

Make the vinaigrette: Into a jar goes the olive oil, red wine vinegar, mayonnaise, oregano, garlic, salt, and a heady amount of pepper. Cap the jar securely and shake it vigorously for 1 minute. It is a workout, but you need to emulsify the mayo into everything else (which gives the dressing extra body). It won't *stay* emulsified, but no biggie. Shake it up when you need it.

Make the salad: Place the lettuce in a large salad bowl. Cut the tomatoes into about 1-inch cubes, and season with the salt. Add the tomatoes, parsley leaves, and pepperoncini to the lettuce. Add vinaigrette to your taste, toss gently, and portion onto plates. Top generously with Parmesan.

TOMATO, PEACH, AND BASIL SALAD

SERVES 4 TO 6

This salad features three things that might sound at odds but I want to show you that you will often find that things can work together if they have friends in common. Imagine that. Anyway, tomato and basil is a well-known pairing. Peaches and basil have a similar affinity. Both tomatoes and peaches are, to varying degrees, sweet and juicy. Put all that together, and voilà! Tomato, peach, and basil salad. The secret weapon is the shaved onion, and a generous seasoning of salt, which ensures that the peaches play a savory role and don't overwhelm with their natural sweetness.

This is a great salad to take to that potluck on Sunday. Or to make as a first course on Saturday. Or to have with some bread and cheese as a simple summer meal any day of the week.

Take a trip to the farmers' market in the summer. Buy some tomatoes, peaches, and basil in their prime. Summer is the time for this dish.

½ large sweet onion, very thinly sliced against the grain

3 heirloom tomatoes (1½ to 2 pounds), cut into 1-inch chunks

3 large peaches, cut into ½-inch slices

Kosher salt

¼ cup Classic Vinaigrette (page 27)

1 cup fresh basil leaves, torn into halves

In a large bowl, combine the onion, tomatoes, and peaches. Season evenly with a couple generous pinches of salt and let sit for 30 minutes; the salt will bring out the juices.

Add most of the vinaigrette and all of the basil to the bowl and toss gently. Taste and add more salt or vinaigrette if the salad still seems too sweet. Serve.

SPINACH SALAD
WITH PEAR, PECANS, BLUE CHEESE

SERVES 4

This is the easy version of the best salad I have ever made in a professional setting. It is hearty and healthy, and follows the number one rule of a great salad: lots of different textures and flavors. Tender spinach, soft sweet pears, crunchy toasted nuts, creamy cheese.

If you're not buying prewashed, clean the spinach in very cold water and spin it dry in a salad spinner or pat it dry with kitchen towels.

The blue cheese here is Gorgonzola, which I find to be one of the mildest blues. You could use a different kind, but try to use a blue that is of really high quality. You don't need much, so it won't be a big investment to get quality dairy goods for this one.

2 tablespoons canola oil

1 cup pecan halves

2 ripe pears

½ cup crumbled Gorgonzola cheese

12 ounces stemmed spinach leaves (if the package is only 11 ounces, so be it)

Kosher salt and freshly ground black pepper

Classic Vinaigrette (page 27)

Set a large skillet over medium heat. Add the canola oil and when the oil is hot, add the pecans. Toast in the pan, stirring often, until the nuts are aromatic and evenly browned, 3 to 4 minutes. Transfer the pecans to a plate lined with a paper towel. When cool enough to handle, chop them up a bit.

Quarter the pears lengthwise and remove the cores. Cut each quarter into three long slices.

In a large salad bowl, combine the pecans, Gorgonzola, pears, and spinach. Season with a couple of pinches of salt and pepper, add vinaigrette to taste (start with 3 tablespoons or so), and toss well. Serve.

THREE-BEAN SALAD

SERVES 4 AS
A MAIN COURSE,
6 AS A SIDE DISH

So if you cooked some dried beans or peas, and have leftovers, as one often does, the next step is to make a three-bean salad. It's a perfect packable lunch, or a great side to a dinner. You can gussy it up easily with some tuna, or cold diced chicken or ham and some toasted sourdough bread, and you have a meal in minutes.

We are going to blanch some green beans for a fresh inclusion in the legume count. Blanching is boiling in salted water until just cooked, and then shocking the vegetable in cold water to quickly arrest the cooking process.

As for the other two beans, you can use navy beans, pinto beans, kidney beans, chickpeas, or really whatever you like, dried or canned. A small can of beans is 15 to 16 ounces, and comes out to about 1½ cups after draining, so I have called for 1½ cups of the main beans to give you flexibility to use canned or home-cooked. If home-cooking, see the method on page 44.

Kosher salt

½ pound fresh green beans, ends trimmed, cut into 2-inch lengths

1½ cups cooked chickpeas (rinsed and drained, if canned)

1½ cups cooked red kidney beans (rinsed and drained, if canned)

2 shallots, thinly sliced into rounds

1 cup thinly sliced celery

1 cup diced peeled cucumber

½ cup chopped fresh flat-leaf parsley

1 tablespoon fresh tarragon leaves

Freshly ground black pepper

½ to 1 cup Classic Vinaigrette (page 27)

Fill a large pot with about 3 quarts water and bring to a vigorous boil over high heat. Add salt until it tastes salty, but not gross.

Set up a bowl of ice and water. Add the green beans to the boiling water and cook until they are just tender and still bright green, for 2 to 3 minutes. Scoop the beans from the pot and add to the ice water to chill. Let them sit until cold. Drain the green beans well. Pat them dry with towels.

In a large bowl, combine the chickpeas, kidney beans, shallots, celery, cucumber, parsley, tarragon, pepper to taste, and ½ cup of the vinaigrette. If you think it needs more vinaigrette, add more. Add the blanched green beans and toss well. Season to taste with kosher salt and toss well again. The salad will keep in the fridge for 5 days.

TOMATO-CROUTON SALAD

**SERVES 4 AS
A SIDE DISH**

Panzanella (Italian bread salad) is a beautiful way to show off big, crisp ripe tomatoes, and basil, all things that should be summer staples in your fo world. With that ever-ready jar of vinaigrette on hand, this comes together pretty quickly and is a great side or satisfying light meal with a hunk of cheese or some cold cuts. It is really important to use good bread.

4 cups torn-up bread pieces

2 pounds tomatoes

2 tablespoons brined capers

2 shallots, thinly sliced into rounds

½ cup Classic Vinaigrette (page 27)

½ cup torn fresh basil leaves

Kosher salt and freshly ground black pepper

Preheat the oven to 400°F.

Place the bread chunks on a sheet pan, transfer to the oven, and toast until the bread pieces are toasty and golden but still soft in the interior, 6 to 10 minutes (bigger pieces will need longer, so keep an eye on them).

Using a paring knife, "core" the tomatoes: Cut down around the stem (or where the stem was) and take out the tough white core and discard. Cut the tomatoes into about 1-inch chunks and place them in a large bowl. Add the capers, shallots, and about half the vinaigrette. Toss well. Add the bread and basil and toss again. Season to taste with salt and pepper and more vinaigrette, if desired. Serve right away.

AND
SANDWICH

...key has been pardoned in this version of a club, and replaced with our Slow-Roasted Soy-Garlic Tofu (page 55), which is delicious with bacon. Yes, you can enjoy tofu *and* meat at the same time, but if you don't eat meat, you can lose the bacon, or use veggie bacon in its place. This sandwich relies on toasting the bread in a large pan, a little vinaigrette to liven things up, and a good amount of mayonnaise to make it the classic it is.

If you are feeling fancy you can get those toothpicks with the frills. Oooh la la.

6 slices good white bread

4 tablespoons mayonnaise

4 slices bacon

1 tablespoon Dijon mustard

1 large red tomato, sliced into rounds

Kosher salt and freshly ground black pepper

4 leaves green leaf lettuce

1 tablespoon Classic Vinaigrette (page 27)

Slow-Roasted Soy-Garlic Tofu (page 55)

Place the bread on a cutting board. Use 2 tablespoons of the mayonnaise to slather evenly on both sides of the bread.

Set a large skillet over medium heat. Add 3 slices of the bread and toast on both sides, using the mayo as the cooking oil. Arrange in a single layer on a cutting board. Repeat with the remaining 3 slices.

Add the bacon to the pan and cook until the first side browns, about 2 minutes, then flip and cook until it's your desired level of crispness or chewiness. Remove the bacon slices to a plate lined with paper towels.

In a small bowl, mix together the remaining 2 tablespoons mayonnaise and the mustard. Evenly slather the mustard-mayo mix on the toasted bread.

Season the sliced tomato with salt and pepper to taste. Set on a plate.

Place the lettuce in a large bowl and toss with the vinaigrette.

To assemble: Lay down 2 slices of bread. Top each with a lettuce leaf and then some tofu and some seasoned tomato. Then top each with another slice of bread. Top those with the rest of the tofu, seasoned tomatoes, bacon, and lettuce. Top that with the final slices of bread. Eat.

GARLIC-SOY TOFU BURRITOS

SERVES 2

This is a basic burrito that tastes great. I always keep tortillas in my home to make tacos or burritos out of nearly anything. Feel free to add sour cream, more salsa, some cheese (and guac if you want, but that will cost extra). You can of course also use meat or scrambled eggs instead of the tofu—or roasted vegetables, like mushrooms. Whatever you put in your burrito, which is a very personal thing, keep these keys to a good burrito in mind:

1. Ingredients are *hot* when they should be.
2. Use a good balance of fresh raw ingredients and cooked ones.
3. Pickled jalapeños are a must. (OK, for me, anyway.)
4. Have everything prepped, hot, and ready to build before you start assembling.
5. Tortillas *must* be warmed to be pliable and delicious!

½ recipe Slow-Roasted Soy-Garlic Tofu (page 55)

½ cup Foolproof Rice (page 41)

½ cup Bacony Black Beans (page 44)

¼ cup chicken or vegetable stock

Kosher salt

1 cup Red Sofrito (page 67)

2 (10-inch) flour tortillas

½ cup grated Monterey Jack cheese

2 cups shredded lettuce

1 cup Pico de Gallo (recipe follows)

Sliced pickled jalapeños

Preheat the oven to 325°F.

Arrange the tofu on a small baking sheet and place in the oven to reheat.

In a small saucepan, combine the rice, beans, stock, and a pinch of salt and warm over medium-low heat, covered, on the stovetop. Stir it once in a while, until hot.

Warm the sofrito in a small skillet or another saucepan, on medium heat, until hot. Take the tofu out of the oven and turn off the oven.

Once the hot stuff is hot, arrange all the ingredients in the order of the recipe.

Set a large skillet over medium heat and griddle one tortilla, flipping it every 10 seconds or so, until hot. Turn off the heat and start the burrito build.

Place the warmed tortilla on a clean flat surface. Place half of the tofu (a plank and a half) in the bottom of the center of the tortilla. Next put half of the rice and beans on the tofu. Then half the sofrito, just slightly in front of the tofu. Then half of the cheese, lettuce, and pico de gallo. Top that pile with the amount of pickled jalapeños that you like. Holding the bottom of the tortilla, fold up the bottom with the bottom edge landing at about the halfway point of the tortilla. Then fold in the sides, and make the finishing roll. Wrap it in foil, if you want. Serve it, or put it in the oven to keep warm.

Reheat the large skillet to heat up the second tortilla and repeat the process.

PICO DE GALLO

MAKES ABOUT 2 ½ CUPS

2 cups diced red tomatoes

½ cup minced red onion

1 tablespoon minced serrano chiles

1 tablespoon minced fresh cilantro

½ teaspoon Diamond Crystal kosher salt, or ¼ teaspoon Morton kosher salt

Mix all together. This will keep, refrigerated, for up to 5 days.

FRIED SHRIMP PO'BOYS

SERVES 4

Saturday afternoon. Football is on. Cold beer. Time for a po'boy.

In terms of using the building block recipes, this recipe calls for the simple slaw from page 65 as a topping for the sandwich. But I'll be honest, I'm including this recipe because I want you to be able to fry food. I didn't write deep-frying as one of the core building block techniques because for a lot of people, the cleanup and days-long scent of fried food in your home make it not feel worth it—and because we shouldn't really eat that much fried food anyway. But whatever. This is really good. Let's make some good food.

1 cup all-purpose flour

1 cup cornmeal

1 tablespoon storebought Cajun seasoning

1 cup buttermilk

1 tablespoon Texas Pete hot sauce

1½ pounds medium shrimp, peeled, deveined, and tails removed

Canola oil, for deep-frying (about 2 quarts)

Kosher salt

4 (8-inch) French or sub-style rolls

1 cup Rémoulade (recipe follows)

2 cups Classic Slaw (page 65)

1 cup shredded iceberg lettuce

8 tomato slices

Freshly ground black pepper

In a medium bowl, whisk together the flour, cornmeal, and Cajun seasoning. Divide it into two bowls. Pour the buttermilk and hot sauce into another medium bowl and mix until fully incorporated. Set the bowls up left to right: cornmeal bowl, buttermilk bowl, cornmeal bowl.

Working in batches, place the shrimp in the first cornmeal bowl and toss to evenly coat. Shake off any excess mixture. Next, place the shrimp in the buttermilk, and coat evenly, then dredge it once more in the second bowl of cornmeal mixture. (If you run out of cornmeal mix in either of the bowls, you can supplement with what's left in the other bowl.) Again, shake off any excess batter, and gently press the batter into the shrimp. Transfer the shrimp to a plate and refrigerate for 20 minutes. This helps the batter stay on the shrimp.

Preheat the oven to warm.

Line a large plate with a couple pieces of paper towel. Into a heavy-bottomed pot that is 6 to 8 inches deep, pour 3 to 4 inches of oil, making sure you have at least 3 to 4 inches to the top of

the pot. Heat the oil over medium-high heat to 375°F. (Use a frying or candy thermometer.)

Split the shrimp into 4 equal batches. Very carefully add 1 batch of the shrimp to the oil; this is best done by lowering the shrimp into the oil (using a spoon or skimmer if you prefer), not dropping it in so that it can splash onto you. Fry, stirring occasionally with a spider skimmer or slotted spoon, until golden brown, 4 to 5 minutes. Use the skimmer to transfer the fried shrimp to the paper towels to drain. As you fry the remaining 3 batches of shrimp, place the cooked shrimp in the oven to keep warm, and season with a pinch of salt. (Try to spread the shrimp out so they are in one shallow layer, not a big pile, which would make them soggy.)

Lightly toast the rolls. Take a healthy amount of rémoulade and smear it all over the inside of the split rolls. Next add the slaw, iceberg lettuce, and tomatoes. Season the tomatoes with salt and black pepper to taste. Finish with the fried shrimp. Serve.

RÉMOULADE
MAKES ABOUT 2 CUPS

1½ cups mayonnaise

¼ cup minced dill pickles

2 tablespoons prepared horseradish

1 tablespoon minced fresh flat-leaf parsley

1 tablespoon Red Sofrito (page 67)

1 tablespoon Dijon mustard

1 tablespoon fresh lemon juice

1 tablespoon hot sauce

1 teaspoon Creole seasoning

1 teaspoon celery seeds

Kosher salt and freshly ground black pepper

In a small bowl, whisk together the mayo, pickles, horseradish, parsley, sofrito, mustard, lemon juice, hot sauce, Creole seasoning, and celery seeds. Season with salt and pepper to taste. This will keep refrigerated for up to 1 week.

GRILLED CHEESE
WITH TOMATO, HAM, AND
SLOW-COOKED ONIONS

SERVES 1

I love tomato on a grilled cheese—the juiciness, tartness, and sweetness of tomato is a great counterbalance to the rich saltiness of the sandwich. (Which, duh, is why tomato soup and grilled cheese is such a classic pairing.) Adding another salty, meaty element—Black Forest ham in this case— is an added bonus. The sweet, melty onions make it a showstopper.

2 slices (½ inch thick) tomato (from a large tomato)

Kosher salt

1 tablespoon unsalted butter, at room temperature

2 slices good-quality bread

3 ounces sliced aged white cheddar cheese

2 ounces thinly sliced Black Forest ham

1 quarter Slow-Roasted Onion (page 59)

Place the tomato slices on a plate. Season lightly with kosher salt and let sit, ideally for 15 minutes. Blot with a paper towel to remove the liquid that the salt has pushed out. Set aside and start your sandwich.

Butter one side of each of the bread slices. Set a large skillet over medium or medium-low heat and when it is hot, place the bread, butter-side down, in the pan. Evenly divide the cheddar between the slices of bread. Toast the bread to golden brown, 3 to 5 minutes, depending on your stove and pan, occasionally peeking to see how the toasting is progressing. The cheese will begin to melt, and once the bread is golden, layer the tomato, ham, and onion on one side. Season the onion with a little pinch of salt. Put the other side of the sandwich on top of it. Reduce the heat to low and cook 1 more minute on one side and then 1 minute on the other, to let the cheese fully melt. Eat.

RICH TOMATO SOUP
WITH BREAD, BASIL, AND OLIVE OIL

MAKES 2½ QUARTS
(SERVES 4 to 6)

This is the convenient version of an Italian soup, pappa al pomodoro, which is a classic tomato soup thickened with bread, almost like a porridge. For our version, we are going to build up base flavor by sautéing onion, adding our core tomato sauce (this is a great way to take excess tomato sauce and make something great!), and then thickening with bread to become a stunningly comforting bowl of soup. The bread in the classic recipe is usually firmed up and, well, stale. This is one of those recipes that almost certainly began, centuries ago, as a way to make something delicious from what would otherwise be waste.

2 tablespoons good extra-virgin olive oil, plus more to finish ✳

½ cup minced yellow onion

4 cups Back-Pocket Tomato Sauce (page 53)

3 cups chicken or vegetable stock

Kosher salt and freshly ground black pepper

4 ounces stale (but good-quality) bread, crust removed, torn into 1-inch pieces

½ cup fresh basil leaves

In a large pot, heat the olive oil over medium-low heat. Add the onion and cook for 7 minutes, stirring every few minutes. The onion should be quite cooked down, but not be very browned. Stir in the tomato sauce and chicken stock. Increase the heat to medium-high and bring to a simmer, then reduce the heat to a gentle simmer and cook for 30 minutes.

Season to taste with salt and add a good amount of pepper. Stir in the torn-up bread and cook for 5 more minutes to thicken. Add the basil leaves, tearing them in half if they are larger than the spoon you will be eating the soup with.

Portion into bowls and drizzle with a good glug of olive oil.

✳ Really good olive oil does not have to be really expensive. Find a brand that you trust—taste it, and if you like the flavor, it's good. Spain, California, Morocco, Portugal, and Italy, among many other places of origin, have wonderful olive oils that are fairly priced. Extra-virgin just means a first pressing of the olives.

119

ctim, a
isadvan-
vilege and
nd live in a
s you like to
truggles of the
, that underdog
other people. You

ng soda before bed?"
alone? I mean—"
k about—"
you have to."

p tonight, most of the night,
een—remember when you were
at creative writing class, and you
s, not two months afterward; you
last breaths even, one paragraph
t breaths, and the whole class kind of
to do with you, they were like, 'We-hell
ether to talk about the story, all of them
with their Xerox copies of it, or to send you
at did not deter you. You have been deter-
get this down, to render this time, to
with it what you hope will be
alking. I've

BUTTERNUT SQUASH AND APPLE SOUP

MAKES ABOUT
1½ QUARTS
(SERVES 4 to 6)

Just like the pureed Leek and Potato Soup (page 80), this warming, sweet-and-savory soup is so easy. It's just a matter of pulling out flavor with a light sauté of vegetables, simmering in stock, and then pureeing to a smooth, luxurious result. You can totally change up the flavor of the soup with a finish (chefs call it "garnish") of anything from country ham to coconut milk. See below for some ideas.

2 tablespoons unsalted butter

½ medium yellow onion, diced

½ cup diced celery

1 Granny Smith apple, peeled and chopped

2 cups large-diced peeled butternut squash (1-inch cubes)

¼ teaspoon ground nutmeg

2 sprigs fresh thyme

2 tablespoons real maple syrup

1 quart chicken or vegetable stock

Kosher salt

½ teaspoon freshly ground black pepper

Garnish of your choice (see suggestions at right)

In a large saucepan, heat the butter over medium heat until it foams up. Add the onion and celery and cook until softening, about 5 minutes. Add the apples, butternut squash, and nutmeg. Cook for 5 minutes and then add the thyme, maple syrup, and stock. Bring to a simmer and adjust the heat so it bubbles but doesn't come to a rolling boil. Cook until the squash is tender, about 30 minutes. Remove from the heat, discard the thyme sprigs, and let cool for 5 minutes before pureeing.

Add half the soup to a blender. Put the blender lid on and remove the center cap/steam vent (or leave the lid open a crack). Holding the lid in place with an oven mitt or towels to protect your hand, blend until smooth. Pour the soup into a bowl or container. Repeat with the rest of the soup. Season to taste with salt and pepper until the flavors really pop.

SUGGESTED GARNISHES

Here are some ideas for garnishes; amounts are to taste:

- chopped scallions and a spoonful of yogurt

- a splash of coconut milk and minced bird's eye chiles

- crème fraîche or sour cream and chopped-up Slow-Roasted Onions (page 59)

- minced country ham and sage leaves sautéed in butter until the butter turns brown

- minced fresh ginger, torn mint, and grated orange zest

PORTUGUESE KALE, POTATO, AND SAUSAGE SOUP

(CALDO VERDE)

MAKES ABOUT 6 CUPS
(SERVES 4)

This soup is winter in a bowl. It is a trip to Portugal for dinner. It's a simple but classic soup, thickened with potato and featuring garlicky sausage and ribbons of tender kale. It takes about 40 minutes to make, and as iconic recipes go, that is speedy. It relies on some skills, which you have, to make it great. Think of this as the same method for a pureed soup, but without the pureeing: The potatoes cook to the point where their starch thickens the soup on its own. The kale provides verdant glory, piqued with two big flavors of Portugal: garlic and a smoky pork sausage called linguiça (if you can't find this, you can use fresh chorizo—as opposed to dried, cured Spanish chorizo—instead).

The kale in this can be whatever you find, but I really like the deep earthy, green flavor of Tuscan kale, also known as dinosaur or lacinato kale. It is pretty commonly available. Mince the stems finely and chop the leaves into bite-size pieces. Never throw away your stems.

¼ cup extra-virgin olive oil, plus more for serving

1 medium yellow onion, minced

4 garlic cloves, very thinly sliced

¼ pound linguiça or Spanish chorizo sausage, cut into ¼-inch rounds

½ pound Yukon Gold potatoes, peeled and diced to ½-inch cubes (store in cold water)

½ pound kale, stems minced, leaves cut into bite-size pieces

1 teaspoon smoked paprika

6 cups chicken stock (low-sodium if you are using store-bought stock)

Kosher salt and freshly ground black pepper

4 large eggs (optional), at room temperature

¼ cup minced scallions

In a heavy-bottomed pot, heat the olive oil over medium heat until shimmering-hot. Add the onion and cook, stirring every minute or so, until translucent, about 5 minutes. Add the garlic and sausage and cook for 3 minutes to bring out their flavor. Drain the potatoes (discard the soaking water), add them to the pot, and keep on cooking for 5 minutes more. Add the kale, paprika, and stock and bring to a boil. Reduce the heat down to a simmer and cook until the potatoes begin to fall apart, 20 to 30 minutes. They will thicken the soup. Season with salt and pepper to taste.

If desired, poach eggs as directed on page 25.

Serve the soup hot with, if you like, a poached egg nestled into each bowl. Finish with a hefty pinch of scallions and a drizzle of olive oil. Leftover soup stores well in the fridge for 5 days or so.

ITALIAN CHICKEN SOUP

MAKES ABOUT 6 CUPS
(SERVES 3 OR 4)

The idea behind this is to mimic Italian wedding soup, which is a clear broth soup with a panoply of vegetables and meatballs. In this case, though, I just want to use roasted chicken. Easier and speedier. This has a fair bit of knife work involved, but relish the prep . . . it should be an enjoyable time. Turn on NPR, listen to a podcast, or put on some music, and soon you'll be sipping a comforting, hearty soup with about a dozen textures to keep you interested.

1 tablespoon extra-virgin olive oil

½ cup minced leek ✳

4 garlic cloves, minced

½ cup small-diced carrot (1 medium carrot)

½ cup small-diced celery (1 medium stalk)

1 teaspoon fresh oregano leaves or a pinch of dried

1½ cups pulled and chopped Roasted Chicken (page 68)

4 cups chicken stock

½ cup orzo pasta

½ cup chopped spinach (frozen is fine, thawed)

½ cup chopped escarole

½ tablespoon freshly squeezed lemon juice

Handful of chopped fresh flat-leaf parsley

2 tablespoons grated Parmesan cheese, or more to taste

Kosher salt and freshly ground black pepper

In a large pot, heat the olive oil over medium heat until shimmering-hot. Add the leek and cook until softening, about 3 minutes. Add the garlic, carrot, and celery and cook, stirring occasionally, until softened but not browned, about 7 minutes.

Add the oregano, chopped chicken, and chicken stock. Bring to a boil, then reduce the heat to a simmer and cook for 10 minutes.

Add the orzo and cook for 15 minutes. Add the spinach and escarole and cook for 5 minutes. Add the lemon juice, parsley, and Parmesan. Remove from the heat and season with salt and pepper to taste. Divide among bowls and finish with more Parmesan, if desired.

✳ Before mincing the leek, trim off and discard the dark green tops, or save for stock, and trim the root end. Halve the leek lengthwise and rinse out any grit that might be hiding between the layers.

BLACK BEAN SOUP
WITH AVOCADO AND SOUR CREAM

MAKES ABOUT 6 CUPS

[SERVES 4 TO 6]

Once you have cooked the beans (or freed them from a can), it can take surprisingly little to turn them into a rewarding, hearty soup. In this case, we'll take cooked black beans and add a flavor-packed tomato-pepper sofrito (which hopefully you already have in your fridge or freezer) and then some creamy avocado and simple garnishes. That's it. If you're not feeling it, you can skip the pureeing step, but doing it adds much more body, as the pureed beans then thicken the rest of the soup.

If you cooked the beans from dried, then save the cooking liquid and use it as a portion, or all, of the stock for this recipe. Better than wasting it, and it tastes great.

1½ tablespoons olive oil

¼ cup Red Sofrito (page 67)

1½ cups cooked black beans, homemade (page 44) or canned (rinsed and drained)

1½ teaspoons finely grated orange zest

3 cups chicken or vegetable stock (or bean broth if you home-cooked beans)

Kosher salt

1 avocado

⅓ cup minced sweet onion

1½ tablespoons freshly squeezed lime juice

3 tablespoons sour cream

In a large saucepan, heat the olive oil over medium-high heat until hot. Add the sofrito and stir for 2 minutes. Add the cooked beans, orange zest, and stock. Bring to a simmer and simmer for 20 minutes. Remove from the heat.

Transfer half of the soup with some beans to a blender. Put the blender lid on and remove the center cap/steam vent (or leave the lid open a crack). Holding the lid in place with an oven mitt or towels to protect your hand, puree until smooth. Transfer the puree to a large bowl. Repeat with the other half of the soup. Season well with salt.

Pit and peel the avocado and cut into cubes (see note, page 117). Ladle the soup into bowls and divide the avocado cubes among them. Garnish with onion, a spoonful of lime juice, and a dollop of sour cream. Serve.

SMOKY WHITE BEAN AND HAM SOUP

MAKES ABOUT
10 CUPS
(SERVES 8)

You have already learned how to cook dried beans into plump, delicious, creamy jewels (see page 44), but here, we'll see what magic you can make just by adding a few flavorful ingredients while the beans are cooking. In this case, a smoked ham hock, some onion, and bay leaves. (Yes, you can really taste them. No, you don't *have* to use them.) From that point we will add stock and vegetables and olive oil and a cascade of Pecorino Romano cheese. It will be great, and even more outstanding the next day. A bean soup in the fridge, ready to reheat, is way more nourishing than ordering Uber Eats. *

2 cups dried white navy beans or other white beans

2 bay leaves

1 smoked ham hock

1 yellow onion, peeled and quartered, plus ½ cup minced

2 cups chicken stock

½ cup finely diced carrot

½ cup finely diced celery

4 garlic cloves, minced

1 tablespoon chopped fresh thyme leaves

2 medium tomatoes, finely chopped, or 1½ cups canned diced

1 cup finely chopped mustard greens or other dark leafy greens

Kosher salt

Extra-virgin olive oil, for serving

Plenty of finely grated Pecorino Romano or Parmesan cheese, for serving

THE DAY BEFORE: Soak the beans as directed on page 45.

DAY OF: Remove the beans from the fridge, drain, and pour into a large pot, adding water to cover by 3 inches. Add the bay leaves, ham hock, and the quartered onion. Bring to a boil over high heat and cook hard for 10 minutes, then cover and simmer over medium-low heat until the beans are just tender, about 2 hours, but check starting at the 1-hour mark.

Once the beans are tender, pull out the ham hock, bay leaves, and onion remnants, keeping the hock, and discarding the bay leaves and onion quarters.

Add the chicken stock, minced onion, carrot, celery, garlic, thyme, and tomatoes to the beans. Increase the heat to medium and cook, uncovered, for 15 minutes. While this is happening, and when the hock is cool enough to handle, remove the meat from the hock, discard any bone and tough sinew, and chop the smoked hock meat finely. Add the meat to the soup and also add the mustard greens. Cook for 5 more minutes and then remove from the heat. Season with kosher salt . . . it may take more salt than you think, as beans tend to need a fair bit to bring out their flavor. At this point you can serve it or chill it for another day.

When ready to eat, garnish each serving with a good glug of olive oil and a heap of grated cheese.

---

* You can halve this recipe, but leftovers are good to have.

SWEET PEA SOUP
WITH YOGURT AND MINT

__MAKES ABOUT 6 CUPS__
__[SERVES 4 TO 6]__

Bright green and fresh, this soup is beloved by all. It is so easy, and uses the best vegetable in the frozen food aisle, frozen peas, simmered quickly and then pureed with potato to enrich the soup. (Certain vegetables really are great frozen—peas and corn especially, since the freezing preserves their sweetness so well.) We finish with a yogurt sauce—the Cucumber Raita on page 86—and the fresh taste of mint. It is great hot or cold, and a cold soup is a perfect portable lunch.

2 tablespoons unsalted butter

1 cup minced yellow onion

½ cup minced celery

1 medium russet potato, peeled and large-diced

4 cups chicken or vegetable stock

8 ounces frozen sweet green peas (aka English peas)

¼ cup loosely packed fresh mint leaves

¼ cup heavy cream

Kosher salt

½ cup Cucumber Raita (page 86)

In a medium pot, melt the butter over medium heat until it foams and bubbles. Add the onion and celery and sweat down the vegetables for about 5 minutes, stirring every minute or so, to develop flavor but not too much color. Add the potato and stock. Increase the heat and bring to a boil, then reduce to a simmer and cook until the potato is tender, 15 to 20 minutes. Add the peas and continue to cook for another 2 minutes to heat through. Add the mint and cream.

Add half the soup to a blender. Put the blender lid on and remove the center cap/steam vent (or leave the lid open a crack). Holding the lid in place with an oven mitt or towels to protect your hand, blend until smooth. Pour it into a bowl or container. Repeat with the rest of the soup.

Season with salt until the flavors really pop. Serve cold or hot with a dollop of raita on each serving.

CREAMY MUSHROOM SOUP

**MAKES ABOUT 6 CUPS
(SERVES 4 TO 6)**

Like the Butternut Squash and Apple Soup (page 147), this is more proof that the same procedure you used for the Leek and Potato Soup (page 80) can produce a totally different product, but with the same velvety texture and satisfying result. In this case, it's the classic woodsy combination of earthy and umami-rich mushrooms, cream, and sherry wine.

Sherry is generally not expensive and choices are abundant, but buy a dry Fino, not a "cooking" sherry. Cooking wines, when labeled as such, have had salt added to them.

4 tablespoons (½ stick) unsalted butter

1 cup minced yellow onion

½ cup minced celery

½ pound cremini mushrooms, chopped

¼ pound shiitake mushroom caps (no stems), chopped

½ pound Yukon Gold potatoes, scrubbed and large-diced

1 cup dry sherry

4 cups chicken stock

1 tablespoon Diamond Crystal kosher salt, or 2 teaspoons Morton kosher salt

1 cup heavy cream

Something to finish: minced chives or parsley, olive oil, dollops of yogurt . . . your call

In a large pot, heat the butter over medium-high heat until it bubbles and froths. Add the onion, celery, cremini, and shiitakes and cook for 10 minutes, stirring every minute or so, to cook out the water from the mushrooms and let them concentrate. Add the potatoes and sherry and stir and cook for 2 minutes. Add the stock and bring to a boil. Add the salt, reduce to a simmer, and cook until the potatoes are cooked through, about 15 minutes. Stir in the cream.

Add half the soup to a blender. Put the blender lid on and remove the center cap/steam vent (or leave the lid open a crack). Holding the lid in place with an oven mitt or towels to protect your hand, blend until smooth. Pour it into a bowl or container. Repeat with the rest of the soup.

Serve hot with some simple garnish like minced chives, a drizzle of olive oil, or some plain yogurt.

SWEET POTATO AND EGGS IN SPICY GREEN TOMATO SAUCE
(SHAKSHUKA)

SERVES 4

This staple egg dish is a crowd-pleaser—eggs baked in tomato sauce—and this version takes on a different profile by using tart green tomatoes in place of red ones, a little hot pepper, salty feta cheese, and bumping up the heartiness with some sweet potato. This is hands down the most rewarding brunch dish you will make in a while, and so easy. If you don't have green tomatoes, feel free to use red, and use whatever cheese you like. The basic idea is what's important here.

2 tablespoons extra-virgin olive oil

1 medium yellow onion, minced

½ poblano pepper, seeded and finely diced

½ jalapeño pepper, seeded and finely diced

2 garlic cloves, minced

1 Baked Sweet Potato (page 39), peeled and diced

½ teaspoon ground cumin

Pinch of cayenne pepper

½ cup cilantro stems, finely minced

2 medium green or red tomatoes, diced, or 1 cup Back-Pocket Tomato Sauce (page 53)

1 cup chicken or vegetable stock

1 teaspoon Diamond Crystal kosher salt, or ½ teaspoon Morton kosher salt

1 cup crumbled feta cheese

8 large eggs

¼ cup fresh cilantro leaves, for garnish

Set a large deep skillet over medium heat. Add the olive oil and onion and cook, stirring occasionally, until the onion is starting to soften, about 5 minutes. Add the poblano, jalapeño, garlic, and sweet potato and cook for another 5 minutes to soften the peppers. Add the cumin, a hearty pinch of cayenne, cilantro stems, and tomatoes and cook for another 5 minutes, then stir in the stock and salt. Sprinkle the feta all over. Let cook for 5 minutes and turn off the heat.

Now, we're going to remove some of the egg whites from the eggs to help the eggs cook to a nice custard-like texture, by upping the ratio of yolk to white, and getting rid of the looser whites. Gather 4 small ramekins or teacups. Working over the sink, gently crack 1 egg in the middle of the shell and remove the top half of the shell, leaving the egg in the other half-shell. Pour the egg into the other half of the shell, and as you do, let some of the whites spill out. Pour the rest of the egg into one of the ramekins. Repeat, filling each ramekin with 2 eggs.

Turn the heat back on under the sauce to medium-low, until the sauce is starting to bubble. Pour each pair of eggs into separate spaces in the sauce, far enough from one another that they don't run all together. Cover and cook until the eggs are just-cooked, about 10 minutes.

Garnish with cilantro leaves and serve the whole pan, letting guests serve themselves in bowls.

ROASTED CARROTS
WITH TOPS, FETA, MINT, AND PICKLED SHALLOTS

SERVES 2 OR 3

If you learned how to roast vegetables on page 61, now you can apply that technique to some of those carrots you see at the store. Not the ones in a plastic bag that look gnarly, but rather the bundle with their green tops still on. We will roast them fast, match them with some of those tops for big green flavor, feta cheese for salty richness, mint for herbaceousness, and some quick pickled shallots for a nice acid bite.

FOR THE PICKLED SHALLOTS
½ cup cider vinegar
1 teaspoon sugar
Kosher salt
2 shallots, cut into thin rings

FOR THE CARROTS
1 pound carrots with tops
1 tablespoon olive oil
Kosher salt

FOR ASSEMBLY
2 tablespoons Classic Vinaigrette
   (page 27)
Kosher salt
½ cup crumbled feta cheese
¼ cup loosely packed fresh
   mint leaves

Preheat the oven to 425°F.

Pickle the shallots: In a small saucepan, combine the vinegar, ½ cup water, the sugar, and a good pinch of salt. Bring to a boil and add the shallots. Remove from the heat and let them sit in the pickling liquid while the carrots roast.

Prep the carrots: Cut the greens from the carrots and pluck off the sprigs of leaves, about 1 inch long, from the tough stems (discard the stems). You need about 1 cup of these greens. (Save the rest to bump up volume in a pesto or a salsa verde.) Immerse the sprigs in a bowl of cold water.

Scrub or peel the carrots and then halve them lengthwise if they are thicker than an inch in diameter. Cut crosswise into 5-inch lengths and place them in a bowl. Toss with the olive oil and season them with a couple pinches of salt. Arrange them on a sheet pan in a single layer and roast until cooked through and caramelized at the edges, 10 to 15 minutes.

To assemble: Drain the carrot greens and dry them in a salad spinner or on a clean kitchen towel. Place them in a small bowl and dress with half of the vinaigrette. Season with a little pinch of salt. Drain the shallots (discard the pickling liquid).

Remove the carrots from the oven and let cool for a couple of minutes. Arrange on a platter and scatter the feta over the carrots. Dot the carrots with mint leaves and dressed carrot tops and finish with pickled shallots. Drizzle some of the remaining vinaigrette around and on the carrots, and serve warm.

ROASTED EGGPLANT
WITH TAHINI, POMEGRANATE, PARSLEY, AND PECANS

SERVES 2

I have spent some time in the Middle East, and fell in love there with a method of grilling eggplants until they are totally soft on the interior, redolent with smoky flavor, and naturally creamy. We can re-create that style at home just with a hot oven. This recipe uses the elements of vegetable roasting on page 61, but is actually a little more akin in technique to baking whole sweet potatoes on page 39.

The tahini sauce is a keeper for many applications. It's a classic of many Middle Eastern cuisines, taking the tahini (imagine peanut butter, but made from sesame seeds) and balancing its richness with lemon juice, and flavoring it with garlic and a little cumin. It's wonderful on roasted broccoli or carrots or at home on some sliced chicken. It is one of those utterly flexible sauces, and it keeps well in the fridge.

1 large eggplant

Kosher salt

½ cup Tahini Sauce (recipe follows)

½ cup pomegranate seeds

½ cup minced fresh flat-leaf parsley

¼ cup chopped roasted unsalted pecans

Arrange a rack in the center of the oven and preheat the oven to 425°F.

Place the eggplant on a sheet pan lined with foil. Roast until the eggplant is very soft, almost collapsed looking, about 45 minutes. It's okay if the skin is charred black, desirable even. Remove the eggplant from the oven and let rest for 10 minutes.

Carefully slice the eggplant lengthwise, place each side on a plate, cut side up, and season with a few sprinkles of salt. Slather the eggplants evenly with the tahini sauce. Pile on the pomegranate, parsley, and pecans and season to taste. Eat, scooping the flesh out if you prefer not to eat the skin.

TAHINI SAUCE
MAKES ABOUT 1 CUP

½ cup tahini

2 garlic cloves, minced

2 tablespoons freshly squeezed lemon juice

¼ cup warm water

¼ teaspoon ground cumin

½ teaspoon kosher salt

2 tablespoons extra-virgin olive oil

In a blender, combine the tahini, garlic, lemon juice, water, cumin, and salt and blend on medium speed. With the machine running, drizzle in the olive oil to emulsify. Use right away, or store in the fridge until needed. It keeps a week or so at peak freshness.

LEEKS
IN SUN-DRIED TOMATO–OLIVE VINAIGRETTE

SERVES 4

We are taking our basic vinaigrette and adding some dynamic notes to it with sun-dried tomatoes, olives, and fresh thyme. This vinaigrette variation is a keeper for salads, to dress roasted vegetables, or is particularly great with chicken or fish. Here we're serving it with leeks braised until meltingly tender, a classic French way to make this gentle cousin of the onion into a delicious dish. This becomes a perfect side for many occasions, and will keep the vegetarians in your fold very happy.

4 leeks

1 tablespoon unsalted butter

½ cup white wine

Kosher salt

½ cup Classic Vinaigrette (page 27)

2 tablespoons minced oil-packed sun-dried tomatoes

2 tablespoons minced pitted Kalamata or other black olives

2 tablespoons minced fresh flat-leaf parsley

1 teaspoon minced fresh thyme leaves

Trim off the dark green tops of the leeks, saving them for a stock. Halve the leeks lengthwise, then rinse them of any grit that might have been hiding between the layers.

Set a large skillet or shallow braising pot (like a Dutch oven) over medium heat. It is important that the pan or pot have a lid, as you will be using it in about 2 minutes. Melt the butter in the pan and add the leeks, wine, ½ cup water, and a couple pinches of salt. Bring it to a simmer, cover, reduce the heat to medium-low, and cook until the leeks are very tender, about 20 minutes. As the leeks are cooking, let's make our gussied-up vinaigrette.

In a small bowl, combine the vinaigrette, sun-dried tomatoes, olives, parsley, and thyme. Mix well to combine.

Remove the leeks from the pan to a platter (discard the cooking liquid). Spoon the vinaigrette over the cooked leeks and serve immediately.

SWEET POTATOES
WITH TOFU, SCALLIONS, AND SOY VINAIGRETTE

**SERVES 4 AS
A SIDE DISH**

Sometimes we can just cobble some of the building block recipes together and make a simple meal that looks very fancy if plated with precision. This is one of those dishes. The sweet potato and tofu add up to a protein and starch combo that works, embellished with scallions and a soy-maple vinaigrette.

¼ cup Classic Vinaigrette (page 27)

1 tablespoon light soy sauce

1 tablespoon maple syrup

6 scallions, thinly sliced

2 Baked Sweet Potatoes (page 39), cooled and peeled

½ recipe Slow-Roasted Soy-Garlic Tofu (page 55), chilled

2 tablespoons canola oil

1 tablespoon toasted white sesame seeds

1 tablespoon fresh lime juice

Kosher salt

In a small bowl, combine the vinaigrette, soy sauce, and maple syrup and stir to blend. Stir in the scallions.

Cut the sweet potatoes into big chunks, but not bigger than your mouth. Cut the planks of tofu into ½-inch cubes.

In a large skillet, heat the canola oil over medium-high heat until hot. Add the sweet potato and tofu and sear for 2 minutes. Turn over each piece to sear for 2 more minutes, until hot through and golden brown.

Arrange the sweet potatoes and tofu on a platter. Spoon the scallion dressing over the potatoes and tofu and then sprinkle sesame seeds over the whole thing. Spritz with lime juice and season with a tiny pinch of salt. Eat.

MAPLE SWEET POTATOES
WITH PECANS AND CHEESE

SERVES 4 AS
A SIDE DISH

I guess most people would think of this as a side dish, but I could eat this as a meal nearly on its own. Anyway, we take the baked sweet potatoes from page 39, and play on them with both sweet (maple syrup) and savory (salty Grana Padano or Parmesan cheese) flavors, and then add pecans for their texture and butteriness. When you have simple food, you can add elements like roasted nuts and salty cheeses to make it more interesting—just always be thinking of things that will bring different textures and counterbalances of flavors, like salty to match sweet, or spicy or sour to match salty, etc.

2 Baked Sweet Potatoes
   (page 39), hot
2 tablespoons unsalted butter
2 tablespoons maple syrup
½ cup crushed roasted unsalted
   pecans
½ cup finely sliced scallions
¼ cup finely grated Grana Padano
   cheese
Kosher salt

After the sweet potatoes have cooked, let them cool for about 5 minutes. Halve them lengthwise and divide the butter evenly among the 4 halves. Drizzle evenly with maple syrup, then sprinkle the pecans over them. Shower with the scallions and then the cheese. Season evenly with a pinch or two of salt, and serve.

FINGERLING POTATOES
WITH GREEN GARLIC VINAIGRETTE

SERVES 4 AS
A SIDE DISH

Roasted young fingerling potatoes get tossed here with the core vinaigrette on page 27 that has been steeping with the springtime glory that is green garlic. Green garlic is the young shoot of what will be a fully formed bulb of garlic. It has a punchy flavor that gives the potatoes a big boost. (If you can't get green garlic, scallions or leeks are a decent substitute.)

The key to this recipe is sautéing aromatics with a little butter and then using that to flavor a vinaigrette. You can take that with you and apply it to other vinaigrettes for roasted vegetables, salads, or to be used as sauces. The butter adds a richness and it mellows the powerful flavor of garlic.

2 pounds fingerling potatoes

2 tablespoons olive oil

1 teaspoon Diamond Crystal kosher salt, or ½ teaspoon Morton kosher salt, plus more for seasoning

1 tablespoon unsalted butter

1 cup minced green garlic (or scallion greens or lighter greens of leeks)

½ cup Classic Vinaigrette (page 27)

Preheat the oven to 400°F.

In a large bowl, toss the potatoes with the olive oil and salt. Spread on a roasting pan and roast the potatoes in the oven for 30 minutes.

While the potatoes are roasting, in a medium skillet, melt the butter over medium heat until it bubbles and froths. Add the green garlic and cook, stirring every minute or so, until soft, about 5 minutes. Season with a pinch of salt and add the vinaigrette. Remove from the heat.

When the potatoes are roasted, put them in a large metal bowl and dress with some of the green garlic vinaigrette to coat. Mix well and serve hot.

HASH BROWNS
WITH GOAT CHEESE AND ROASTED RED PEPPERS

<u>SERVES 4 AS A SIDE</u>
<u>DISH OR 2 AS A MEAL</u>
<u>WITH A SALAD</u>

This ample side is a meal when matched with a little salad. You take crisp hash browns and top them with goat cheese, scallions, and roasted peppers, then bake them to a melting result. It is so easy to assemble once the hash browns are made, and so good.

Hash Browns (page 32)

½ cup chopped roasted red bell pepper, homemade (see ↑ on page 67) or jarred

2 tablespoons minced scallions

Kosher salt

4 ounces fresh goat cheese

Preheat the oven to 375°F.

Place the cooked hash browns on a sheet pan. In a small bowl, mix together the roasted peppers and scallions and season with a pinch of salt. Pile evenly on the hash browns. Crumble the goat cheese evenly over the roasted peppers.

Transfer to the oven and bake for 10 minutes. If you want, turn the oven to high broil and broil the tops to get some color on the cheese, a minute or two. Remove from the oven and serve.

HASH BROWNS
WITH SMOKED SALMON AND THINGS THAT GO WITH SMOKED SALMON

**SERVES 4 AS A
LIGHT MEAL WITH A
SALAD OR A SIDE**

When I think of smoked salmon, I think of a bagel with cream cheese, capers, shaved red onion, fresh dill, a smidge of lemon juice, and a generous grind of black pepper. We're taking that ideal brunch and using crisp, hot hash browns instead of the bagel. But you could just as easily swap out those items for tiny gherkins (pickles), toasted caraway, and salmon roe. Or yogurt, sour cream, or crème fraîche.

Smoked salmon can be a pricy treat, but you don't need a lot of it to make a satisfying meal: It's so flavorful you can eat a lot of potatoes (or bagels, or toast) with it. But you could also use less expensive smoked fish here—smoked trout is wonderful, or smoked whitefish, etc.

Hash Browns (page 32)
Kosher salt
8 ounces sliced smoked salmon
¼ cup Cucumber Raita (page 86)
¼ red onion, thinly sliced
2 tablespoons brined capers
¼ cup chopped fresh dill
½ lemon, for squeezing
Freshly ground black pepper

Place the freshly finished hash browns on a cutting board while they are still piping hot and season with salt. Dividing evenly, drape the salmon over the hash browns. Spoon some raita over the salmon and arrange onion and capers over that, evenly and with a light touch. Dot with fresh dill, squeeze a bit of lemon over, and generously grind pepper over the finished product. Eat immediately.

CURRY SPINACH AND TOFU
(SAAG PANEER, KINDA)

SERVES 2

Saag paneer is an Indian stew of spinach, spices, and pressed cubes of fresh cheese. It's delicious, and while this dish isn't exactly saag paneer, it's inspired by it. We use the slow-roasted tofu from page 55, which has a texture similar to paneer cheese, and it comes together quickly. For the spinach, use frozen and you will have very consistent results.

3 tablespoons canola oil

4 garlic cloves, finely minced

2 shallots, minced

1 tablespoon minced fresh ginger

1 serrano chile, seeded and minced

1 tablespoon Madras curry powder

½ cup vegetable stock or water

½ cup plain whole-milk yogurt

1 pound frozen spinach, thawed

1½ cups Slow-Roasted Soy-Garlic Tofu (page 55), cut into ¼-inch dice

1 tablespoon freshly squeezed lime juice

Kosher salt

2 cups Foolproof Rice (page 41, ideally using basmati), hot *

In a large, deep sauté pan, heat the canola oil over medium heat until shimmering. Add the garlic, shallots, ginger, and serrano and cook, stirring, until slightly browned and aromatic, about 2 minutes. Add the curry powder and continue cooking until the spices are very aromatic. Add the stock and yogurt. Add the spinach and cover with a lid. Reduce the heat to low and cook for 10 minutes.

Add the diced tofu, sprinkle in the lime juice, and season with salt until it tastes delicious. Serve with the rice.

---

* If using leftover rice, microwave or sauté over medium heat with a touch of oil until steaming-hot.

SEARED SUMMER SQUASH
WITH MINT AND VINAIGRETTE

**SERVES 2 TO 4
AS A SIDE DISH**

This is a great way of treating tender vegetables—give them a good sear and then dress them while still hot to absorb flavor. Your dressing and flavorings and vegetables can vary to your taste, but the method can be one you can draw on over and over. Try this with asparagus, sugar snap peas, even green beans.

Summer squash includes zucchini, yellow squash, little pattypans, crooknecks, and many others. For this recipe, look for squash about 8 inches long and 2 inches in diameter, weighing 6 to 8 ounces per piece. This method will sear them, just on one side, on really high heat. Then they will get seasoned and sit in that hot pan to mellow out, with the heat off. Off to the side I am going to add mint, pepper flakes, and lemon zest to our core vinaigrette from page 27, and then all will get tossed together. It is a great side, hot or cold. Don't worry about making too much, as it is a great packed-lunch component the next day.

Grapeseed is a high-quality neutral oil. It is a "high-heat" oil, which means it has a high smoke point and can get really hot before it starts to break down and have off flavors (extra-virgin olive oil would have a burnt oil taste when cooked at this heat). You can also use a simple, not-roasted peanut oil or extra-light olive oil for this kind of searing.

3 straight yellow summer squash or zucchini, 8 inches long and 2 inches wide (6 to 8 ounces each)

1 tablespoon grapeseed or other high-heat oil

Kosher salt

½ cup lightly packed fresh mint leaves

½ teaspoon crushed red pepper flakes

½ teaspoon finely minced lemon zest (see ✳, page 189)

¼ cup Classic Vinaigrette (page 27)

Freshly ground black pepper

Trim the ends off the squash and then cut the squash into big bite-sized chunks.

Heat a large, heavy skillet over high heat. Add the grapeseed oil and when you see it lightly smoke, carefully add the squash pieces to the pan cut-side down, making sure they all sit flat on the pan. Sear without disturbing them, until the bottom is nicely browned, about 3 minutes. Remove the pan from the heat, season the squash with a few pinches of salt, and let them sit while you assemble the remaining step.

Mince up the mint leaves and place them in a large bowl. Add the pepper flakes, lemon zest, vinaigrette, and a good amount of black pepper. Add the cooked squash while still hot and toss well. Serve.

SWEET POTATO HASH
WITH SALSA ROSSA AND SOUR CREAM

SERVES 2

A hash is a natural landing place for a fried, scrambled, or poached egg (page 25), a beautiful side to some roasted chicken (page 68), or a simple meal all by itself, maybe gussied up with some chunks of ham or sausage and a salad on the side. This one adds the flavors of onion, peppers, and some tomato sauce and sour cream. Using the whole baked sweet potatoes as a starting point gets this on the table in just a few minutes. Of course, if you use a regular baked potato in this recipe, you can have a more traditional hash instead.

2 tablespoons canola oil, plus more if needed

2 cups peeled and cubed Baked Sweet Potatoes (page 39)

1 medium yellow onion, small-diced

1 red bell pepper, diced

2 tablespoons Salsa Rossa (page 84)

2 tablespoons sour cream, plus more for serving

1 tablespoon sliced scallions

1 tablespoon chopped fresh flat-leaf parsley

Kosher salt and freshly ground black pepper

In a large, heavy skillet, heat the oil over medium heat until shimmering-hot. Add the sweet potato, spread it out to a single layer, and cook, undisturbed, until a good amount of golden brown color has developed on the bottom, 6 to 8 minutes.

Add the onion and bell pepper and stir to combine. Add a splash of oil if the pan seems dry. Continue cooking, stirring occasionally, until the onions and peppers are softened, about 4 minutes.

Add the salsa rossa, sour cream, scallions, and parsley. Season to taste with salt and black pepper and mix again. Cook for about 1 more minute to set the hash.

Serve garnished with a nice dollop of sour cream and some freshly ground black pepper.

ROASTED CHICKEN LETTUCE WRAPS
WITH HERBS

SERVES 2 TO 4

Fresh and easy should be just that. If you have some roasted chicken (page 68), pork shoulder (page 48), or roasted tofu (page 55) already cooked, then this crunchy, crisp, meaty, satisfying recipe takes about 10 minutes to get done, assuming your knife skills are pretty speedy. The sauce, Nuoc Cham (page 87), is a classic Vietnamese condiment/sauce/dip you should have in your fridge at all times; it makes just about anything taste great.

2 cups minced cold Roasted Chicken (page 68)

1 shallot, minced

1 tablespoon minced fresh ginger

1 tablespoon rice vinegar

1 tablespoon roasted peanut oil

1 tablespoon fish sauce

1 teaspoon toasted sesame seeds

Kosher salt

10 Bibb lettuce leaves

1 cup julienned carrot

1 cup julienned cucumber

½ cup minced scallions

6 sprigs fresh cilantro

12 fresh mint leaves

1 cup Nuoc Cham (page 87)

In a bowl, combine the minced chicken, shallot, ginger, vinegar, peanut oil, fish sauce, and sesame seeds. Mix well and then season with a pinch or two of salt. Mix again and set aside.

Arrange the lettuce leaves on a work surface. Evenly divide the chicken mixture into the lettuce leaves, then evenly distribute the carrot, cucumber, scallions, cilantro, and mint leaves onto the chicken piles. Serve nuoc cham on the side. Eat them like tacos, splashing on the sauce with a spoon.

STRIP STEAK, ONION PUREE, AND SPINACH

SERVES 2

Soubise is a French sauce that is a creamy puree of onions. Here, we will make a super-easy version of it by pureeing the slow-roasted onions from page 59 with cream. It's a simple sauce that makes you look like a total pro, a natural match with a steak, but also a good one for fish or chicken. It is earthy and sweet, rich but not too rich.

We'll serve it with a beautiful steak, and some spinach wilted in the steak's fat. Get cooking.

½ recipe Slow-Roasted Onions (page 59)

1 cup heavy cream

Kosher salt

1 New York strip steak, 1 inch thick, 12–16 ounces

4 cups loosely packed spinach leaves (any tough stems removed)

In a blender, combine the onions, cream, and a few generous pinches of salt and puree until smooth. Place the onion puree in a small saucepan and heat over medium heat, stirring occasionally, until hot. Taste, add more salt if desired, then remove from the heat and cover. (Leftover soubise can be refrigerated for about 5 days.)

Cook the steak as directed on page 72. When the steak is done, remove it to rest, but leave the pan on the stove.

Place the steak pan over medium heat, add the spinach, and turn it around a lot with some tongs. Season with a pinch of salt. Cook for 1 to 2 minutes, until it is just wilted down. Remove the spinach and blot on a couple of sheets of paper towel over a plate if it seems a bit too fatty.

Spoon about ¼ cup (that's 4 tablespoons) of the onion sauce on the center of each of two plates. Arrange the spinach in the center of each pool of sauce. Slice the steak and arrange on the spinach. Serve.

POACHED EGGS
WITH SOFRITO, BUTTERED KALE, AND GRITS

SERVES 2

Sofrito is the flavor base I want you to have on hand at all times. Cook some more tomatoes with it and you have an intriguing tomato sauce. Slather it on a crisp-skinned chicken thigh and you have something you'll crave. And use it by itself as a sauce, and you can add enough flavor to pantry basics to make a meal.

Here, we're going to build a dish of sautéed, buttered kale and poached eggs with grits.

1 cup Red Sofrito (page 67)
1 tablespoon olive oil
4 cups torn kale leaves
Kosher salt
Pinch of crushed red pepper flakes
1 teaspoon unsalted butter
1 teaspoon freshly squeezed lemon juice
4 large eggs
2 cups cooked grits, hot (page 77)

In a small saucepan, warm the sofrito over low heat for 5 minutes. Cover and just let it do its thing, stirring once in a while.

Set a large skillet over medium-high heat and add the olive oil. When the oil is shimmering-hot, add the kale and cook, stirring occasionally, for 3 minutes. Season with a pinch of salt, remove from the heat, and add the pepper flakes, butter, and lemon juice. Stir well to coat the kale. Put a lid on the pan to keep warm.

Poach the eggs as directed on page 25. Divide the sofrito and grits between two serving bowls. Pile kale equally into the bowls. Nestle 2 eggs onto each pile of kale. Eat.

STEAK
WITH HASH BROWNS, MUSHROOMS, AND WARM VINAIGRETTE

SERVES 2

This is a great dish, but in terms of it being a recipe, it's really just an assemblage of four of the basic building blocks at the beginning of this book. So this is really more of a game plan for you, one that can help get you comfortable with the kind of timing it takes to put together a meal. (And some of the ways you can be efficient.) You'll want to make the hash browns and steak fresh, since the potatoes lose their crispness if they're hanging around too long, and the steak is best hot. But the vinaigrette you could have premade for days; same with the mushrooms. So it's just a matter of reheating some things while you finish up. The herbs aren't strictly necessary, but they add a delicious complexity; use them as you wish.

½ cup Classic Vinaigrette (page 27)

1 cup Sautéed Mushrooms (page 31), cool or at room temperature

1 Butter-Basted or Pan-Roasted Steak (page 72)

½ recipe Hash Browns (page 32)

¼ cup fresh basil leaves

¼ cup fresh flat-leaf parsley leaves

1 tablespoon fresh tarragon leaves

1 tablespoon chopped fresh rosemary

Make the vinaigrette and sautéed mushrooms ahead.

Preheat the oven to 400°F.

Cook the steak and the hash browns at about the same time, using two burners. If you'd feel more comfortable doing one at a time, I would suggest doing the hash browns first, then setting them aside.

When the steak is removed from the pan to rest, add the mushrooms to the steak pan, still with its cooking juices and crusty bits. Add the vinaigrette and place in the oven for 3 minutes to warm the mushrooms through. If you made the hash browns first, pop them back in the oven for a few minutes to rewarm and recrisp, too.

Plate by placing a hash brown on each plate and then the steak, sliced if you want. Remove the mushrooms from the oven, add the herbs, toss lightly, and spoon this evenly over the plates of steak.

SALMON AND LEMON-MINT RICE
WITH RAITA AND LETTUCES

SERVES 2

This is a kind of restaurant-style dish that is really just a plate filled with a mix of basic building block recipes: the Pan-Roasted Salmon (page 75), Foolproof Rice (page 41), and Cucumber Raita (page 86).

We are going to finish the rice with preserved lemon, which has a big bold flavor and a fair bit of mint—meaning a lot. (If you can't get preserved lemon, don't let that stop you from making the dish; you can season the rice with a squeeze of lemon juice instead in a pinch.)

The lettuces will be a crisp addition, dressed with the raita, which we also use as a sauce for the entire dish.

2 cups Foolproof Rice (page 41), made with basmati
½ cup chicken or vegetable stock
¼ preserved lemon
½ cup chopped fresh mint leaves
Pan-Roasted Salmon (page 75)
2 cups mixed small lettuces
1 cup Cucumber Raita (page 86)
Kosher salt

In a small saucepan, combine the cooked rice and stock and warm it over medium-low heat, stirring to help it heat up evenly. You're not trying to cook it more, so once it's hot enough to eat, turn off the heat.

Thoroughly rinse the preserved lemon under fresh water, squeeze dry, remove the pulp, and then finely mince the remaining skin and pith. Stir the minced lemon and the mint into the rice and set aside in a warm place until ready to serve.

Divide the rice between two plates. Perch a salmon fillet on the rice. Dress the lettuce leaves with half of the raita. Season with a pinch of salt and put them on the plates. Spoon the remaining raita on the plates next to the rice.

POACHED EGG, POLENTA, PANCETTA, PARMESAN

SERVES 4

I didn't set out to make a dish with four P's, but now it's here to stay: warming, comforting, full of salty, umami flavors and the luxuriousness of an oozy egg. Brunch or dinner, this will make you happy anytime.

Pancetta is rolled and cured pork belly from Italy. When thinly sliced it looks like little pinwheels. It has a robust porky cured flavor that is wonderful, like a funky, unsmoked bacon. You can find it in the deli section of most grocery stores. Ask for it thinly sliced.

Parmigiano-Reggiano is the real-deal Parmesan cheese and is the classic ingredient that shows the difference between the apex of quality and the rest of the herd. There are so many "Parmesan cheeses," but only one Parmigiano-Reggiano. It's not cheap and it shouldn't be; but a little goes a long way and it's worth the splurge if you can afford it. I shave it with a peeler, pulling away in thin lengths to adorn the polenta.

As for the other two P's, I trust you have studied them enough on pages 25 and 77.

8 thin round slices pancetta

4 large eggs (at room temp if possible)

Soft Polenta (page 77), reheated if necessary ✱

Kosher salt

4 ounces Parmigiano-Reggiano cheese, shaved

Extra-virgin olive oil, for drizzling

Preheat the oven to 400°F.

Arrange the pancetta in a single layer on a sheet pan. Bake until it is crisp, about 10 minutes. Remove the pan from the oven and transfer the cooked pancetta with tongs to a couple of layers of paper towel to wick away the grease.

Poach the eggs as directed on page 25.

Spoon a generous serving of soft polenta onto each plate. Center a poached egg on each pile of polenta and season with a pinch of salt. Perch 2 slices of pancetta over the egg. Shower with shaved Parmigiano and drizzle with a touch of olive oil.

✱ If you are using leftover polenta from the fridge, you will need to reheat it in a saucepan with a few splashes of water to get it soft again. Cook it over medium-low heat with a few tablespoons of water and stir constantly (a whisk might make it easier). Add water as needed and taste if you need to add more salt.

ROASTED CHICKEN
WITH RADICCHIO, CAPERS, EGGPLANT, AND CRISP BREAD

SERVES 4

This is a simple chicken recipe that comes out looking like you are a fancy chef with a fancy restaurant in the fancy part of town. Impress your friends. If you have followed the book in a linear fashion, this is easy. You've roasted chicken (page 68), you've sautéed greens (page 63), you've made croutons (page 117). We're just putting 'em all together here, so the juices soak into the crisp bread. If you haven't, this is still easy.

Roasted Chicken (page 68)

⅓ cup plus 2 tablespoons extra-virgin olive oil

2 cups cubed or torn bread (about ½-inch cube-like shapes)

Kosher salt

2 cups peeled and diced (think thumbnail size) eggplant (from 1 large eggplant)

1 shallot, minced

1 garlic clove, minced

1 tablespoon unsalted butter

8 ounces radicchio, cored and chopped

2 tablespoons salt-packed capers, rinsed

1 tablespoon grated lemon zest ✳

Freshly ground black pepper

Prep the chicken and get it into the oven as directed.

Meanwhile, set a large skillet over medium heat. Add ⅓ cup of the olive oil to the pan and wait about 20 seconds for it to heat up. Add the bread and just keep an eye on things. Try to give a little space between the pieces. They will begin to brown after about 2 minutes. Move them around, turning them with a spoon. Season with a couple of pinches of salt. Continue cooking until they are all toasty and golden, about 5 minutes total. Remove to paper towels to wick away any excess oil. Wipe out the pan.

When the chicken is a few minutes away from being ready—maybe while it's resting—add the remaining 2 tablespoons olive oil to the skillet and set it over medium heat. Wait for the oil to shimmer, then add the eggplant. Sear, turning after a few minutes, until the eggplant is golden brown on most sides, 6 to 8 minutes.

Add the shallot and garlic and cook for 2 more minutes. Add the butter and let it melt until it starts to foam, then add the radicchio, capers, and lemon zest. Gently stir until the radicchio slightly wilts. Don't cook it all the way down, just until warmed through. Season with salt and pepper to taste and mix with the toasted bread.

Carve the chicken by removing the legs, separating the thigh from the drumstick, and then removing both sides of the breast and cutting them into two or three pieces each.

Arrange the vegetables and the bread on a large platter. Then lay the roasted chicken pieces on top and serve.

✳ Using a vegetable peeler, peel off strips of lemon zest (just the yellow layer, not the white underneath). Finely chop the strips until you have 1 tablespoon. Or use a zester.

SKILLET MEATLOAF
WITH TOMATO GLAZE AND SWEET ONION SLAW

SERVES 4

This recipe may look a little bit more intense than some of the others, but most households in this country have made a successful meatloaf a part of their regular eating routine, and you should, too. It's not hard, even if it looks like a lot of ingredients. You're basically blending most of it up and baking it; the result is a juicy meatloaf with a sweet/tart/savory sauce painted on, and some beautiful crunchy, sweet slaw.

FOR THE GLAZE
½ cup Red Sofrito (page 67)
2 tablespoons packed light brown sugar
½ cup cider vinegar
½ teaspoon freshly ground black pepper

FOR THE MEATLOAF
1 slice bread, crusts removed and torn into rough pieces
4 ounces white mushrooms
2 tablespoons unsalted butter
2 medium garlic cloves, minced
1 medium onion, minced
½ cup minced carrot
½ cup minced celery
1½ pounds ground beef (80% lean/20% fat)
¼ cup finely minced fresh flat-leaf parsley
1 large egg
1 tablespoon Diamond Crystal kosher salt, or 2 teaspoons Morton kosher salt
1 teaspoon paprika
Freshly ground black pepper
1 tablespoon canola oil

FOR SERVING
Sweet Onion Slaw (recipe follows)

Arrange an oven rack in the lowest position and preheat the oven to 375°F.

First let's prepare the glaze: In a blender, combine the sofrito, brown sugar, vinegar, and black pepper and puree until smooth. Transfer to a small saucepan and cook over medium-low heat until it has thickened enough to coat the back of a spoon, about 10 minutes. Remove from the heat and set aside.

Make the meatloaf: In a food processor, coarsely chop the torn bread and mushrooms. (If you don't have a food processor, chop them to the best of your ability with a knife and board.) Set the bread and mushroom mixture aside.

In a large skillet, heat the butter over medium heat until it starts to foam. Add the garlic, onion, carrot, and celery and cook the vegetables until softened, about 5 minutes. Transfer to a pan or plate to cool.

In a large bowl, combine the beef, mushroom mixture, cooled vegetables, parsley, egg, salt, paprika, and pepper to taste. Mix really well, until the beef is tacky and sticky. (This gives it a more bouncy, dense bite.)

In a 10-inch cast-iron skillet or other ovenproof skillet, heat the canola oil over medium heat until shimmering-hot. Spread the meatloaf mixture evenly in the pan, then place the skillet on a sheet pan (so it doesn't make a mess in your oven) and put the whole thing in the oven. Roast for 20 minutes, then pull the meatloaf out of the oven and evenly spread ½ cup of the glaze over it. Return to the oven and cook until the internal temperature reaches 145° to 150°F on a meat thermometer, usually 10 to 20 minutes longer.

Let the meatloaf rest for 10 minutes, then cut into wedges and serve with the sweet onion slaw.

SWEET ONION SLAW

MAKES ABOUT 2¼ CUPS

1 cup Classic Slaw (page 65)

1 cup chopped Slow-Roasted Onions
   (page 59)

¼ cup sliced scallions

Kosher salt and freshly ground
   black pepper

In a bowl, combine the slaw,
onions, and scallions. Season with
salt and pepper to taste.

STEAK SALAD
WITH GREEN PAPAYA

<u>SERVES 2 TO 4</u>

This is inspired by some of the seminal flavors of Vietnam, where green papaya salad is often made with a kind of beef jerky.

Green papaya is an unripe papaya, and is crunchy and refreshing and not sweet; its flavor is probably closest to a cucumber or a kohlrabi. It is inexpensive and available in most larger grocery stores or markets specializing in Asian foods.

The basic cooking blocks you will use in this are many: cooking steak, vinaigrette, and from the simple sauces block, the delightful punch of the Nuoc Cham—a classic, savory-sour-sweet all-purpose sauce in Vietnam that can make anything delicious. You can enjoy this salad as a meal all on its own, or with a scoop of hot jasmine rice (page 41).

1 New York strip steak

1 small green papaya (about 1 pound), peeled, halved, and seeded

½ cup thinly cut carrot rounds

1 cup thinly sliced red onion

¼ cup fresh mint leaves, chopped up a bit

2 tablespoons chopped fresh cilantro

1 tablespoon minced jalapeño pepper

¼ cup roasted unsalted peanuts

¼ cup Nuoc Cham (page 87)

¼ cup Classic Vinaigrette (page 27)

Kosher salt

2 cups Foolproof Rice (optional; page 41), for serving

Pan-roast the steak and let it rest as directed on page 72. After resting, place on a plate and put it in the fridge.

Shred the papaya finely ✱, spaghetti-like in width. Place it in a large bowl and add the carrots, onion, mint, cilantro, jalapeño, and peanuts. Slice the steak thinly against the grain. Add it to the papaya and vegetables in the bowl. In a mason jar, combine the nuoc cham and vinaigrette and shake to combine. Liberally dress the salad with about half the dressing. Toss well, season with salt to taste, add more dressing if desired, and serve with rice on the side for a meal.

✱ When I say shred it, you have choices: You can use (1) a knife to cut off slices and then finely julienne it, (2) a julienne attachment on a food processor, (3) a Japanese mandoline with a julienne blade, or (4) a wavy vegetable peeler, which has a blade with ridges that produces julienne strands; it's super inexpensive and handy to have.

PORK AND CHILE CHICKPEA STEW
WITH OR WITHOUT POACHED EGGS

**MAKES ABOUT
12 CUPS
[SERVES 4 TO 6]**

If you have leftover Slow-Roasted Pork Shoulder (page 48)—and, unless you are a dinosaur, you probably will—and you have cooked chickpeas (page 44, or canned), the delicious marriage of the two is a speedy meal. The stew is brightened with chile and tomato, and takes a turn to fresh and zesty with cilantro and lime. Since I am a lover of poached eggs, I'd put them on this, too, but that's up to you. And if you have more pork than chickpeas in your fridge or vice versa, you can just use more of one or the other depending on what you have. This makes about 3 quarts of stew, which means you'll have dinner and a few lunches, ready to heat up.

2 tablespoons canola oil

1 medium yellow onion, minced

1 cup minced celery

6 garlic cloves, minced

2 tablespoons ancho chile powder

1 teaspoon ground cumin

¼ cup canned chopped green chiles

2 cups canned tomato puree

4 cups chicken stock

1½ cups cooked chickpeas, homemade (page 44) or 1 (15-ounce) can, rinsed and drained

2 cups packed chopped Slow-Roasted Pork Shoulder (page 48)

4 to 6 large eggs (optional)

1 cup loosely packed chopped fresh cilantro

2 tablespoons freshly squeezed lime juice

Kosher salt

In a large pot, heat the canola oil over medium heat until hot. Add the onions and celery and cook, stirring occasionally, until very soft, about 10 minutes. Add the garlic, ancho powder, cumin, and green chiles. Cook for 5 minutes, stirring, then add the tomato puree, stock, chickpeas, and pork. Bring to a boil over high heat. Reduce to a simmer and cook, stirring every few minutes, for 45 minutes. Everything should look like it is coming together into a stew consistency.

If desired, poach the eggs as directed on page 25.

Stir the cilantro and lime juice into the stew and season to taste with salt. Serve with a poached egg nestled into each bowl, if desired.

PORK TACOS
WITH CABBAGE SLAW

SERVES 4

Once you have cooked pork, like shreds from the beautiful roasted pork shoulder on page 48, tacos are a natural destination. Match them with some slaw, for crunch and balance, a zippy salsa, and some lime and you have a party.

Canola oil

1½ pounds Slow-Roasted Pork Shoulder (page 48), shredded (about 3 cups packed)

Kosher salt

12 corn tortillas

1 medium red onion, minced

2 cups crumbled Cotija cheese

2 cups Classic Slaw (page 65)

4 limes, cut into wedges

Tomatillo Salsa Verde (recipe follows)

Set a large skillet over medium heat. Add 1 tablespoon canola oil and add the pork. Cook the pork for about 8 minutes, turning often, getting it crisped up nicely. Season to taste with a pinch of kosher salt. Remove the pork from the pan and place in a bowl, covered with foil, as you warm the tortillas. (Or place it in the oven, set to warm.)

Clean out the skillet, return it to medium heat, and very lightly film it with some canola oil. Griddle the tortillas for 20 to 30 seconds per side until warmed through. As you proceed through the tortillas, place them in a resealable plastic bag to stay warm; or use a clean, folded kitchen towel to keep them snug in a blanket.

Put the crisped pork into a serving vessel and serve with the warm tortillas, the minced onion, Cotija, cabbage slaw, lime wedges, and tomatillo salsa verde, plus any other toppings you love on a taco.

TOMATILLO SALSA VERDE
MAKES 2 CUPS

Tomatillos aren't tomatoes, but they are related. They're tangy and green, with a bright fresh flavor, and come covered in a papery husk. Just peel the husk, rinse off any stickiness if necessary, and chop.

2 cups coarsely chopped tomatillos

½ cup minced sweet onion

1 cup packed fresh cilantro stems and leaves

2 tablespoons freshly squeezed lime juice

1 teaspoon ground cumin

1½ tablespoons thinly sliced seeded serrano chiles

1 tablespoon extra-virgin olive oil

Kosher salt

In a blender, combine the tomatillos, onion, cilantro, lime juice, cumin, serranos, and olive oil and puree until smooth. Season with salt to taste. This can be prepared ahead of time and will keep refrigerated for up to 1 week.

STEAMED MUSSELS
WITH SOFRITO

SERVES 2 TO 4

Mussels seem out of reach for many of us, but are really easy to cook, and are easier to prepare than clams, for instance, because they are almost always farmed and brought in clean, without sand. And they're often cheap. They have a great, sweet flavor of the ocean and just need a quick, steamy bath and they'll open right up.

When you buy mussels, they should smell like the ocean, not fishy. They should be tightly shut or, if open, should close quickly when tapped on a countertop, as if you are trying to wake them up. Get rid of any that don't close. Figure on ¾ to 1 pound per person as a main course.

This recipe uses a flavorful tomato-pepper red sofrito as a base and some dry vermouth—which you should have around in case someone ever asks for a martini—and a good amount of bread for sopping up the broth.

2 tablespoons unsalted butter

2 shallots, minced

1 cup Red Sofrito (page 67)

1 cup dry vermouth

2 pounds fresh mussels, debearded ✱

Kosher salt

½ cup thinly sliced scallion rounds

4 slices great bread

In a large lidded pot, heat the butter over medium-high heat until it bubbles and froths. Add the shallots and cook, stirring, to soften, about 2 minutes. Add the sofrito and cook until it bubbles. Add the vermouth and the mussels. Cover and cook until all of the mussels have opened, about 8 minutes. (You can peek at about 5 minutes to see how things are going; once they're open, they're done.) If there are one or two that just refuse to open, just move on and call it, saving the other 39 souls from being overcooked. You want to get them out of the heat quickly after they open. Discard the ones that have not opened.

Taste the broth and season with salt if it's not already popping with flavor. Add the scallions, toss well, and serve, dividing the broth and mussels among the bowls. Serve with bread.

✱ I clean mussels by purging them in a couple of changes of cold, salty water, and then removing any barnacles and sea things that have become attached to the shells. They also should be "debearded," which means using your fingers to pull out the little stringy "beards."

STEAMED CLAMS
WITH MUSHROOMS, COCONUT MILK, AND CHILES

SERVES 2

Clams cook just like mussels. Steam them in some nice tasty stuff for a few minutes and they open. If they are not opening, and are really tightly closed, that just means that you have found very fresh clams, and will need to cook them longer than normal. But in general, the two are interchangeable in terms of recipes, and though they taste different from each other, they are both deliciously briny. And most recipes for them follow the same general pattern: Start with some fat or oil and some aromatic ingredients, add some liquid and the shellfish, let them cook, and it's dinnertime.

This version combines the meatiness of mushrooms (from page 31) with a little bit of hot chile, coconut milk, and the clams' own broth. It is a simple and easy recipe full of spice and freshness. Serve with some bread or hot rice for sopping up that broth.

Manila clams are smaller clams that are raised on the West Coast. They are plump and tender, and tend to have the best meat-to-shell ratio of commonly available clams. "Purging" clams means to give them a chance to expel any dirt that remains within them. This is done by soaking them in cold salted water, which gives them a taste of home. A vigorous swirling will help them open up and get that dirt out.

1 tablespoon unsalted butter

1 shallot, minced

1 tablespoon minced fresh ginger

1 cup Sautéed Mushrooms (page 31)

1 cup vegetable stock

1 bird's eye chile, very thinly sliced

2 pounds fresh Manila clams

1 cup canned full-fat coconut milk (shaken in the can)

Kosher salt

¼ cup minced fresh cilantro

1 tablespoon freshly squeezed lime juice

Bread or rice, for serving

Get a big pot on the stove and melt the butter over medium-high heat until bubbling and frothy. Add the shallot and ginger and cook for 1 minute. Add the cooked mushrooms, vegetable stock, chile, and clams. Cover and cook for 3 minutes.

Add the coconut milk and cook until all the clams have opened, 5 to 7 more minutes. (Discard any clams that have not opened.) Season to taste with salt, focusing on the broth's salinity more than anything.

Stir in the cilantro and lime juice. Serve the clams as a shared dish in a big bowl, or in individual servings, with slices of bread or with rice on the side.

ROASTED CHICKEN SALAD

SERVES 4

Chicken salad is something that is really good to have in your Monday morning fridge. It will give you a great lunch as a sandwich, a quick dinner with some roasted broccoli and toasted bread, or just a snack on some crackers. The trick is to make it light and herbaceous, and that is accomplished with a mix of yogurt and mayo, lemon, and tarragon and parsley—the tartness of yogurt and lemon brighten up the flavor, and the herbs keep it interesting. So simple and so good.

The chicken can be leftovers from Roasted Chicken (page 68). There is always leftover roasted chicken and there is always a use for that roasted chicken.

½ cup mayonnaise

½ cup plain whole-milk Greek yogurt

2 tablespoons freshly squeezed lemon juice

2 tablespoons chopped fresh tarragon leaves

2 tablespoons minced fresh flat-leaf parsley

½ teaspoon crushed red pepper flakes

2 teaspoons Diamond Crystal kosher salt, or 1¼ teaspoons Morton kosher salt

1 cup diced seeded peeled cucumber

½ cup roasted unsalted almonds, crushed a bit

3 cups pulled and chopped Roasted Chicken (page 68)

In a large bowl, combine the mayonnaise, yogurt, lemon juice, tarragon, parsley, pepper flakes, and salt. Mix well (a whisk helps). Add the cucumber, almonds, and chicken. Stir well and serve. Will keep in the fridge for 4 days.

ROASTED CHICKEN
WITH CORN, SLOW-ROASTED ONIONS, AND TOMATO SALAD

SERVES 4

Summer is a beautiful time for food that doesn't take all day to cook, but simply harnesses what the season is all about. Corn, tomatoes, onions, and roasted chicken are an amazing quartet to make that happen. If you have the slow-roasted onions from page 59 hanging out in your fridge like I do much of the time, this comes together in about 5 minutes once your chicken is cooked.

Roasted Chicken (page 68)

2 cups corn kernels
(from 2 to 3 ears corn) ✱

½ cup chopped Slow-Roasted Onions
(page 59)

1 cup cherry tomatoes, halved

1 tablespoon coarsely chopped fresh
tarragon

1 teaspoon ground fennel

1 tablespoon Classic Vinaigrette
(page 27)

Kosher salt and freshly ground black
pepper

Roast the chicken as directed, and while it is resting, make the salad: In a bowl, mix together the corn, onions, tomatoes, tarragon, fennel, and vinaigrette. Season generously with salt and pepper, tasting as you go.

Carve and serve the chicken with the corn salad.

✱ To cut the kernels off fresh corn, first peel back the papery husks and pull off the silky threads. (You can rub them off with a paper towel if pulling them off seems like a chore.) Put the ear of corn down on a cutting board pointing away from you. With a sharp knife, slice off one side of the kernels. Turn the cob so it's lying on the flat side and slice another side of kernels off. Repeat until you have all the kernels. For extra credit, take your knife and scrape the cob, running all the way down, to get out all the milky juice.

CHICKEN AND DUMPLINGS

SERVES 4

This is modern comfort food with a Southern accent—traditionally, dumplings are soft and pillowy and cooked in a rich chicken stew, and the modern part is topping it with a bright, acidic, herbal salsa verde from page 85, loaded with the crunch of celery. And we make it convenient here by using leftover roasted chicken from page 68 as our base.

Still, this can seem like one of the more involved recipes in this book, and it is, but I want you to get comfortable with mixing the dough for the dumplings. It's easy, and it will make you feel like you really accomplished something from scratch.

FOR THE DUMPLINGS

2 cups all-purpose flour

1 teaspoon baking powder

1 teaspoon baking soda

1 teaspoon Diamond Crystal kosher salt, or ½ teaspoon Morton kosher salt

1 tablespoon cold unsalted butter, small-diced

¾ cup buttermilk

FOR THE CHICKEN STEW

2 tablespoons unsalted butter

3 tablespoons canola oil

2 medium yellow onions, diced

4 garlic cloves, minced

⅓ cup all-purpose flour

4 cups chicken stock

3 cups shredded Roasted Chicken (page 68)

Kosher salt and freshly ground black pepper

1 cup Celery Salsa Verde (recipe follows)

Celery leaves and buttermilk, for garnish (optional)

Make the dumplings: In a medium bowl, mix the flour, baking powder, baking soda, and salt. Toss the butter in the flour mixture and mash with a fork, to achieve a crumbled texture. Fold in the buttermilk and mix just until smooth. Be careful not to overmix, as that would make the dumplings chewy. Chill for 1 hour in the fridge.

Make the stew: In a large pot, melt the butter and canola oil over medium heat. Add the onions and garlic and cook until they start to soften, about 4 minutes. With a heatproof silicone spatula or wooden spoon, stir the flour in and cook over medium-low heat until it looks like it's become a matte coating on the onions, about 2 minutes. Switch to a whisk and stir in the chicken stock, making sure all the flour gets incorporated, so we get a smooth finished product.

Bring the stock to a boil, stirring often. Once it's at a boil, reduce to a simmer and add the shredded chicken. Season to taste with salt and pepper. I tend to go a little heavy-handed on the black pepper with chicken and dumplings; it just seems like a perfect pair. Simmer for 15 minutes, then remove the stew from the heat and set aside until you're ready to make the dumplings.

To poach the dumplings, bring the stew back to a simmer over medium heat and start adding spoonfuls of the dumpling batter to the hot stock. Think the size of golf balls. Repeat until all the batter is used. Stirring gently, allow the dumplings to cook until fluffy and cooked all the way through, 10 to 12 minutes.

Ladle the stew and dumplings into bowls and garnish with celery salsa verde and, if desired, celery leaves and a drizzle of buttermilk.

CELERY SALSA VERDE

MAKES ABOUT 1 CUP

¾ cup Salsa Verde (page 85)

⅓ cup minced celery

2 pinches of celery seed

Kosher salt and freshly ground
   black pepper

In a small bowl, mix together the
salsa verde, minced celery, and
celery seed. Season with salt and
pepper to taste.

RIB-EYE STEAK
WITH SALSA VERDE, ESCAROLE, AND PICKLED CHILES

SERVES 2

In this recipe we will take a rib-eye steak and pair it with some of the staple salsa verde from page 85 that you should keep in the fridge for times you need a tart, savory, vegetal sauce. Then we'll stew down some escarole with butter and enliven that with pickled chiles. Once your steak is cooked, this whole thing is done in just a few minutes.

Escarole is a type of endive, but leafy and large, unlike the bullet smoothness of a Belgian endive. It's like a hearty lettuce that cooks well, has a beautiful bitterness that mellows when cooked, and pairs perfectly with butter and a smidge of lemon. The pickled chiles will give us some heat and punch, but meld well with the escarole.

This will sound odd, but if you can't find escarole, iceberg lettuce is a great substitute. It just has a more timid flavor.

1 (14-ounce) rib-eye steak

2 tablespoons unsalted butter

4 cups chopped escarole or Belgian endive leaves, cleaned of grit ✱

1 tablespoon freshly squeezed lemon juice

Kosher salt

2 tablespoons chopped Pickled Chile Rings (recipe follows)

½ cup Salsa Verde (page 85)

Cook the steak as directed on page 72 and let it rest. Meanwhile, cook the escarole.

In a large skillet, heat the butter over medium-high heat until it melts, bubbles, and froths. Add the escarole and cook until lightly colored, wilted, and buttery, about 3 minutes. Add the lemon juice and season with a few pinches of salt to taste.

Slice the steak and place on a platter. Arrange the escarole next to the steak with the chiles and then streak the steak with salsa verde. Serve.

✱ To clean the escarole of grit, use the rinsing method described in the first step of Garlic Sautéed Swiss Chard (page 63).

PICKLED CHILE RINGS
MAKES ABOUT 2 CUPS OF CHILES IN BRINE

4 red Fresno chiles

1 cup cider vinegar

1 tablespoon sugar

1 teaspoon Diamond Crystal kosher salt, or ½ teaspoon Morton kosher salt

Slice the chiles in rings, discarding the stems. Place the rings in a medium heatproof bowl.

In a small saucepan, combine the vinegar, 1 cup water, sugar, and salt and bring to a vigorous boil over high heat.

Pour this pickling brine over the chiles and let sit for 1 hour. These will keep in the fridge, in the brine, for a few weeks.

SEARED CATFISH
WITH CHILE-TOMATO-COCONUT BROTH

<u>SERVES 4</u>

Catfish is a definite value, and is a sustainable choice in the world of seafood. Buy American catfish, as it's the good stuff and an important part of our aquacultural economy. It's delicious, meaty, and not at all muddy tasting, despite what you might have heard. Now that I've said that, you can make this dish with other kinds of fish as well. And whatever you use, this will be great.

This recipe uses the basic fish pan-roasting technique as is used for the salmon on page 75, but just on one side. After the single-sided sear, we put together a broth in the pan, and then the fish is finished in it, with the seared side facing up. It is so easy and efficient. The ingredient list looks long, but the results are great, a combination of Thai and not-so-Thai flavors. Star anise is a spice that appears a lot in Vietnamese cooking and is a staple in pho broth. It is a unique and very interestingly delicious flavor, sort of a cross between cinnamon and licorice. Just make sure to pluck it out of the finished dish. If you can't get it, make the dish anyway.

2 tablespoons canola oil

4 catfish fillets (about 5 ounces each)

Kosher salt

2 small shallots, sliced into thin rings

1 tablespoon minced fresh ginger

1 whole star anise

⅓ cup Back-Pocket Tomato Sauce (page 53)

⅓ cup chicken stock

½ cup coconut milk (preferably full-fat, shaken in the can)

1 tablespoon Thai red curry paste

1 tablespoon light brown sugar

1 tablespoon fish sauce

½ cup fresh basil leaves, hand-torn

1 cup fresh cilantro sprigs, hand-torn

4 cups Foolproof Rice (page 41, ideally using jasmine rice), hot

Lime wedges, for serving

Line a plate with paper towels. In a large sauté pan, heat the canola oil over medium heat until shimmering-hot. Pat the fish very dry with paper towels, lightly season it with kosher salt, and add it to the pan, leaving some room between the fillets. Gently press down on the fillets with a spatula or spoon for the first 30 seconds or so, and sear until golden brown, 2 to 4 minutes. Transfer the fish to the paper towels.

Set the sauté pan over medium-low heat. Add the shallots, ginger, and star anise to the pan and cook for 2 minutes. Add the tomato sauce, chicken stock, coconut milk, curry paste, brown sugar, and fish sauce and bring to a boil. Reduce the heat to a simmer and cook for 15 minutes, stirring occasionally. Remove the star anise. Double-check the seasoning and add salt if needed.

Return the fish to the pan of simmering broth and cook until the fish's rubbery translucency has turned into tender flakes of fish, about 3 minutes—the time of this really hinges on how thick your catfish is: A thin fillet will take less time.

Transfer the fish to a platter and spoon a generous amount of broth over the fish. Garnish with basil and cilantro. Serve with hot rice and lime wedges.

PORK POZOLE

SERVES 8

Pozole is a hearty Mexican stew or soup made with the same kind of corn that is used to make tortillas (called *pozole* in Spanish and *hominy* in English). It's not the sweet corn you eat on cobs; it's hard and starchy with a tough skin, made edible by an ancient process called nixtamalization, and you can buy it canned. It has a flavor somewhere between a potato and popcorn. It is a keeper.

This stew uses that corn, and some of the flavors it's often paired with in Mexico—dried chiles, onion, cumin, and sweet spices—and is also a wonderful use of the slow-roasted pork shoulder from page 48, which always makes enough for leftovers. As with so many stews in this book (and in life), if you don't have pork but have chicken or other meat, it can go right in instead.

A guajillo chile is a dried Mexican chile that is a beautiful dark red. It's medium-hot, but has terrific flavor. You soak it and then blend it to make the base flavor for this stew.

4 guajillo chiles

2 tablespoons canola oil

1 large red onion, diced

1 cup diced carrot

1 cup diced celery

2 teaspoons ground cumin

1 teaspoon ground coriander

2-inch cinnamon stick

2 tablespoons fresh oregano, chopped

2 quarts chicken stock

1½ cups cooked pinto beans, homemade (page 44) or canned (rinsed and drained)

4 cups chopped Slow-Roasted Pork Shoulder (page 48)

2 cups canned hominy, rinsed and drained

Kosher salt

½ cup chopped fresh cilantro with finely cut stems

Avocado, chopped, for serving

Lime wedges, for squeezing

16 tortillas, warmed, for serving

Stem and seed the guajillos and chop them into 1-inch-long pieces. Soak them in warm water to cover for 30 minutes. Reserving 1 cup of the soaking water, drain the chiles and transfer to a blender. Blend the chiles with the reserved soaking water.

In a large pot, heat the canola oil over medium-high heat. Add the onion, carrot, and celery and cook, stirring occasionally, until they're softening, about 5 minutes. Add the cumin, coriander, cinnamon stick, and oregano. Cook for 2 minutes to meld the flavors, then add the chicken stock, pinto beans, chopped pork, guajillo puree, and hominy. Bring to a simmer, then reduce the heat to maintain the simmer and cook for 30 minutes. Season to taste with kosher salt.

Divide into bowls and garnish with the chopped cilantro and avocado. Serve with lime wedges for squeezing and some warm tortillas. Great the next day as well and will keep for 1 week in the fridge.

CHICKEN TORTILLA CHIP STEW
(CHILAQUILES)

SERVES 2

I always keep tortillas in my fridge; a quick warm-up in a hot, dry skillet and I can taco or quesadilla anything. Some leftover meat? Taco it. Roasted vegetables and some cheese? Quesadilla it. But sometimes your tortillas get a touch stale, or you just want something else to do with them. Well, if you haven't had chilaquiles you are missing something beautiful. You crisp them up in the oven (or fry them or . . . honestly, you can also use quality tortilla chips for this). You make a sauce, full of fresh cilantro and tomato and chiles (in our case, we're taking the sofrito from page 67 you have in your fridge and amping it up), and then you add the crisped tortillas to it. They soften slightly and make a hearty and zesty nacho-like stew, which is garnished with sour cream, pickled jalapeños, cilantro, lime, and shaved onion. This recipe is so warmly spicy and comforting, and you can sub in really any protein for the chicken as well.

4 (5-inch) round corn tortillas (or a few big handfuls of hearty tortilla chips)

2 tablespoons canola oil

Kosher salt

1 shallot, minced

2 cups Red Sofrito (page 67)

1 cup chicken stock

1 cup chopped Roasted Chicken (page 68)

½ cup minced fresh cilantro

½ teaspoon ground cumin

1 tablespoon freshly squeezed lime juice

GARNISHES

Sour cream

Cilantro leaves

Shaved red onion

Avocado slices

Pickled jalapeños

Lime wedges, for squeezing

Preheat the oven to 325°F (or skip this step if you're using premade chips).

Tear the tortillas into bite-size pieces. Place them in a bowl and toss them with 1 tablespoon of the canola oil. Season with a pinch of salt and spread them on a sheet pan in a single layer. Transfer to the oven and toast until crisp, about 12 minutes.

In a large skillet, heat the remaining 1 tablespoon canola oil over medium heat. Add the shallot and cook for 3 minutes. Add the sofrito, chicken stock, and chopped chicken and cook for 5 minutes, so it's bubbling and the flavors come together. Add the cilantro, cumin, and lime juice.

Season to taste with salt. Mix to combine and then add the toasted tortilla pieces (or tortilla chips), stirring to fully coat them. Let sit for a minute to come together.

Divide the chilaquiles onto plates. Garnish with sour cream, cilantro leaves, shaved red onion, avocado, pickled jalapeños, and a lime wedge. Serve.

STEAK SALAD
WITH PICKLED RADISHES AND SOY VINAIGRETTE

SERVES 2 TO 4

This is so good, so easy, and just works every time. Crunchy, tender, meaty, and satisfying.

Thinly sliced steak is served with quick-pickled radishes and the basic vinaigrette from page 27, made with soy and ginger. The lettuces I use in this are Bibb, Boston, or Butter. The three B's are tender and are readily available in grocery stores.

1 New York strip steak, 1 inch thick, weighing 12 to 16 ounces

6 small red radishes, cleaned and greens removed

1 cup rice vinegar

1 teaspoon Diamond Crystal kosher salt, or ½ teaspoon Morton kosher salt

1 teaspoon sugar

½ cup Classic Vinaigrette (page 27)

1 tablespoon soy sauce

1 tablespoon minced fresh ginger ✱

1 head Bibb lettuce, torn into bite-size pieces

Pan-roast the steak and let it rest as directed on page 72. After resting, place on a plate and put it in the fridge.

Slice the radishes in ¼-inch-thick rounds and put them in a heatproof bowl. In a small saucepan, combine the rice vinegar, 1 cup water, the salt, and sugar. Bring to a boil, then pour it over the radishes. Let sit for a while, ideally 1 hour.

Place the vinaigrette in a mason jar, add the soy sauce and ginger, seal with a lid, and shake well.

Remove the steak from the fridge and thinly slice against the grain, removing any sinew and excess fat that you wouldn't want to eat. Divide the steak slices among serving plates.

Drain the radishes (discard the pickling liquid) and place them in a medium salad bowl. Add the lettuce. Dress with the vinaigrette to taste and toss gently. Drizzle some more vinaigrette over the steak slices. Dividing evenly, arrange the dressed lettuces and radishes on the steak plates, and serve.

✱ You can peel fresh ginger easily just by scraping it with a spoon. A 1-inch piece or so should give you about 1 tablespoon minced.

POT ROAST
WITH CELERY ROOT PUREE AND POMEGRANATE-PARSLEY SALAD

SERVES 4

Paired with a pomegranate and parsley salad (or any bright, tart salad), this tender braised beef is a great winter dish. If you've made the pork shoulder on page 48, then this is easy. If not, it is still easy. (This is the same as the braised pork method except that there is no dry rub used and we will switch up the flavors.)

In terms of what to buy for pot roast, you can actually use a number of different cuts, almost all inexpensive. Expensive cuts, like steak, have little or no sinew, but braising melts tough sinew, turning the meat deliciously tender. So not only do you get a very delicious dish out of this, you get it for cheap.

2-pound boneless chuck roast

2 teaspoons Diamond Crystal kosher salt, or 1 teaspoon Morton kosher salt, plus more to taste

Freshly ground black pepper

1 tablespoon canola oil

1 tablespoon unsalted butter

4 garlic cloves

¾ cup dry red wine

2 cups beef stock

5 small red creamer potatoes, halved

1 celery stalk, cut into 4 lengths

2 medium carrots, quartered lengthwise

1 medium turnip, quartered

4 ounces white mushrooms

2 fresh bay leaves

4 sprigs fresh thyme

Pomegranate-Parsley Salad (recipe follows)

Celery Root Puree (recipe follows)

Arrange an oven rack in the lowest position and preheat the oven to 275°F. Pat the beef dry with paper towels. Season all over with the salt and pepper to taste.

Set a heavy ovenproof pot, like a Dutch oven or soup pot, large enough to fit the beef in, over medium-high heat. Add the oil and butter and when the oil is hot, add the roast and sear for 3 minutes on each side, to get a nice brown crust. Add the garlic cloves and wine and let it cook until the wine reduces by half. Add the beef stock, potatoes, celery, carrots, turnip, mushrooms, bay leaves, and thyme.

Cover the pot, transfer to the oven, and cook until the meat is not falling apart, but is tender enough for a fork to pierce through it easily, 1½ to 2 hours. Take the pot out of the oven, remove the bay leaves, and allow the meat to rest for about 30 minutes before slicing.

Serve the pot roast with the pomegranate salad and celery root puree.

POMEGRANATE-PARSLEY SALAD

SERVES 4 AS A GARNISH

1 cup pomegranate seeds

1 cup fresh flat-leaf parsley leaves

1 tablespoon Classic Vinaigrette (page 27)

Freshly ground black pepper

In a bowl, toss together the pomegranate seeds, parsley, vinaigrette, and pepper to taste.

CELERY ROOT PUREE

SERVES 4

2 cups diced peeled celery root

1 cup whole milk

½ teaspoon Diamond Crystal kosher salt, or ¼ teaspoon Morton kosher salt

2 tablespoons unsalted butter, cold and cubed

In a large saucepan, combine the celery root, milk, and salt and bring to a boil over medium-high heat. Reduce to a simmer and cook until the celery root is tender, 15 to 20 minutes.

Drain the celery root in a colander set over a bowl and reserve both. Transfer the celery root to a blender along with enough cooking liquid to cover one-third of the cooked celery root. Not adding too much liquid is key to a good puree; there is a fine line between a puree and soup.

Put the blender lid on and remove the center cap/steam vent (or leave the lid open a crack). Holding the lid in place with an oven mitt or towels to protect your hand, puree on a low speed, then increase it to high. If the blender is having trouble "catching" and creating a vortex, add a little more of the cooking liquid until it is running smoothly. While the blender is running, add the butter and puree for 30 more seconds. Double-check the seasoning. It should be ready to go. Keep warm in a covered small pot until ready to use.

ACKNOWLEDGMENTS

Books don't just happen without a cohesive team of people dedicating hours to the task at hand. Andrew Thomas Lee took the pictures, let us invade his kitchen, and was such a gracious host. Thanks to Kate and Alice for enduring countless leftovers and missing spoons. Thanks to Sam Herndon for being the cooking wizard that he is. Thanks to Francis Lam for being a patient yet sharp editor, guiding the book into something we could all be proud of. The Clarkson Potter/Random House team is a group of total pros: Sonia Persad, Stephanie Huntwork, Mark McCauslin, Heather Williamson, and Nick Patton design and produce books with grace. To Doris Cooper and Aaron Wehner, thanks for running the best cooking imprint in the land.

And, as always, this book doesn't happen without the love of my wonderful kids, Beatrice and Clementine. You got this. Go cook some food.

INDEX

A

Apple and Butternut Squash Soup, 147
Avocado Toast with Feta and Roasted Broccoli, 120

B

Bacon
  Bacony Black Beans, 44–45
  and Poached Egg Salad, 118
  and Roasted Tofu Club Sandwich, 138
Basil
  Pesto, Spaghetti with, 113
  Tomato, and Peach Salad, 130
Bean(s). *See also* Chickpea(s)
  Black, Soup with Avocado and Sour Cream, 152
  dried, cooking, 42–45
  Pork Pozole, 211
  Three-, Salad, 134
  White, and Fennel Salad, 124
  White, and Ham Soup, Smoky, 155
Beef
  Burgers, 35–37
  Butter-Basted or Pan-Roasted Steak, 71–73
  Luxe Patty Melt with Slow-Roasted Onions and Pickles, 128
  Pot Roast with Celery Root and Pomegranate-Parsley Salad, 216
  Rib-Eye Steak with Salsa Verde, Escarole, and Pickled Chiles, 207
  Skillet Meatloaf with Tomato Glaze and Sweet Onion Slaw, 190
  Spaghetti and Meatballs, 96
  Steak Salad with Green Papaya, 193
  Steak Salad with Pickled Radishes and Soy Vinaigrette, 215
  Steak with Hash Browns, Mushrooms, and Warm Vinaigrette, 182
  Strip Steak, Onion Puree, and Spinach, 180
Black peppercorns, 15
Bread. *See also* Crouton(s)
  Basil, and Olive Oil, Rich Tomato Soup with, 145
  Crisp, Radicchio, Capers, and Eggplant, Roasted Chicken with, 189
Broccoli
  Roasted, 61
  Roasted, and Feta, Avocado Toast with, 120
Brunoise, defined, 19
Burgers, 35–37
Butter, Clarified, 33

C

Cabbage
  Slaw, Pork Tacos with, 197
  Slaw: Simple and Classic, 64–65
  Sweet Onion Slaw, 191
Carrots, Roasted, with Tops, Feta, Mint, and Pickled Shallots, 161
Catfish, Seared, with Chile-Tomato-Coconut Broth, 208
Celery
  Pine Nuts, and Cheese, Iceberg Salad with, 126
  Salsa Verde, 205
Celery Root Puree, 217
Cheese
  Avocado Toast with Feta and Roasted Broccoli, 120
  Blue, Pear, and Pecans, Spinach Salad with, 133
  Cavatelli with Chickpeas, Tomato Sauce, Ricotta, and Basil, 108
  Celery, and Pine Nuts, Iceberg Salad with, 126
  Chef's Salad, 117
  Goat, and Roasted Red Peppers, Hash Browns with, 170
  Grilled, 56–57
  Grilled, Cuban, 125
  Grilled, with Pear and Slow-Cooked Onions, 121
  Grilled, with Tomato, Ham, and Slow-Cooked Onions, 144
  Luxe Patty Melt with Slow-Roasted Onions and Pickles, 128
  and Pecans, Maple Sweet Potatoes with, 167
  Poached Egg, Polenta, Pancetta, and Parmesan, 186
  Roasted Carrots with Tops, Feta, Mint, and Pickled Shallots, 161
  Wheat Berry Salad with Tomato, Feta, Mint, and Olives, 107
Chicken
  carving directions, 70
  and Dumplings, 204
  Gussied-Up Instant Ramen, 95
  Louisiana-Style Dirty Rice with Greens, 99
  and Potato Salad with White Wine and Herbs, 123
  Roasted, 68–70
  Roasted, and Grits with Broth and Poached Eggs, 92
  Roasted, Lettuce Wraps with Herbs, 178
  Roasted, Salad, 202
  Roasted, with Corn, Slow-Roasted Onions, and Tomato Salad, 203
  Roasted, with Radicchio, Capers, Eggplant, and Crisp Bread, 189
  Soup, Italian, 151
  Tortilla Chip Stew, 212
Chickpea(s)
  dried, cooking, 44–45
  and Pork Chile Stew with or without Poached Eggs, 194
  Three-Bean Salad, 134
  Tomato Sauce, Ricotta, and Basil, Cavatelli with, 108
Chile(s)
  Nuoc Cham, 87

Pork Pozole, 211
Red Sofrito, 66–67
Rings, Pickled, 207
-Tomato-Coconut Broth, Seared
    Catfish with, 208
Chop, defined, 19
Clams, Steamed, with Mushrooms,
    Coconut Milk, and Chiles, 201
Corn, Slow-Roasted Onions,
    and Tomato Salad, Roasted
    Chicken with, 203
Crouton(s)
    Pan-Fried, 117
    -Tomato Salad, 137
Cucumber Raita, 86
Curry Spinach and Tofu, 173
Cutting terms, 19

D

Dice, defined, 19

E

Eggplant
    Radicchio, Capers, and Crisp
        Bread, Roasted Chicken with,
        189
    Roasted, with Tahini, Pomegranate,
        Parsley, and Pecans, 162
Egg(s)
    Gussied-Up Instant Ramen, 95
    Poached, 24–25
    Poached, and Bacon Salad, 118
    Poached, and Broth, Roasted
        Chicken and Grits with, 92
    Poached, Polenta, Pancetta, and
        Parmesan, 186
    Poached, Pork and Chile Chickpea
        Stew with or without, 194
    Poached, with Sofrito, Buttered
        Kale, and Grits, 181
    and Sweet Potato, in Spicy Green
        Tomato Sauce, 158
Equipment, 17
Escarole
    Italian Chicken Soup, 151
    Poached Egg and Bacon Salad, 118
    Salsa Verde, and Pickled Chiles,
        Rib-Eye Steak with, 207

F

Fennel and White Bean Salad, 124
Fish
    Hash Browns with Smoked Salmon
        and Things That Go with
        Smoked Salmon, 171
    Pan-Roasted, 74–75

Salmon and Lemon-Mint Rice with
    Raita and Lettuces, 185
Seared Catfish with Chile-Tomato-
    Coconut Broth, 208

G

Garlic
    Oil, 84
    and Olive Oil, Spaghetti with, 91
    -Soy Tofu, Slow-Roasted, 54–55
    Green Garlic Vinaigrette, Fingerling
        Potatoes with, 168
Green Papaya, Steak Salad with, 193
Greens. See also specific greens
    Louisiana-Style Dirty Rice with, 99
    Poached Egg and Bacon Salad,
        118
    Sautéed, 62–63
Grits
    and Roasted Chicken with Broth
        and Poached Eggs, 92
    Sofrito, and Buttered Kale,
        Poached Eggs with, 181
    Soft, 76–77
Grocery shopping, 9–11

H

Ham
    Chef's Salad, 117
    Cuban Grilled Cheese, 125
    Tomato, and Slow-Cooked Onions,
        Grilled Cheese with, 144
    and White Bean Soup, Smoky, 155
Herbs, 15–16. See also specific herbs
    Celery Salsa Verde, 205
    Salsa Verde, 85

I

Ingredients
    complementary flavors, 11–14
    cutting terms, 19
    shopping for, 9–11

J

Julienne, defined, 19

K

Kale
    Buttered, Sofrito, and Grits,
        Poached Eggs with, 181
    Potato, and Sausage Soup,
        Portuguese, 148
Kimchi
    and Pork, Fried Rice with, 114

and Sausage, Crisped Rice with,
    103
Knives, 18–19
Kosher salt, 16

L

Leek(s)
    and Potato Soup, 78–81
    and Shrimp, Spaghetti with, 104
    in Sun-Dried Tomato–Olive
        Vinaigrette, 165
Lettuce
    Chef's Salad, 117
    Classic Green Salad, 28–29
    Iceberg Salad with Celery, Pine
        Nuts, and Cheese, 126
    and Raita, Salmon and Lemon-
        Mint Rice with, 185
    Red Check Salad, 129
    Steak Salad with Pickled Radishes
        and Soy Vinaigrette, 215
    Wraps, Roasted Chicken, with
        Herbs, 178

M

Meatballs, Spaghetti and, 96
Meatloaf, Skillet, with Tomato Glaze
        and Sweet Onion Slaw, 190
Mince, defined, 19
Mushroom(s)
    Coconut Milk, and Chiles,
        Steamed Clams with, 201
    Hash Browns, and Warm
        Vinaigrette, Steak with, 182
    Sautéed, 30–31
    Soup, Creamy, 157
Mussels, Steamed, with Sofrito, 198

N

Noodles. See Ramen
Nuoc Cham, 87
Nuts. See Pecans; Pine Nuts

O

Olive–Sun-Dried Tomato
        Vinaigrette, Leeks in, 165
Onion(s)
    Puree, Strip Steak, and Spinach,
        180
    Slaw, Sweet, 191
    Slow-Cooked, and Pear, Grilled
        Cheese with, 121
    Slow-Cooked, Tomato, and Ham,
        Grilled Cheese with, 144
    Slow-Roasted, 58–59

Onion(s), *cont.*
  Slow-Roasted, and Pickles, Luxe Patty Melt with, 128
  Slow-Roasted, Corn, and Tomato Salad, Roasted Chicken with, 203
  Slow-Roasted, Pork, and Apples, Polenta with, 111

P

Pancetta, Poached Egg, Polenta, and Parmesan, 186
Parsley
  -Pomegranate Salad, 216
  Salsa Verde, 85
Pasta
  Cavatelli with Chickpeas, Tomato Sauce, Ricotta, and Basil, 108
  cooking, 50–51
  Italian Chicken Soup, 151
  Spaghetti and Meatballs, 96
  Spaghetti with Basil Pesto, 113
  Spaghetti with Garlic and Olive Oil, 91
  Spaghetti with Shrimp and Leeks, 104
  with Tomato and Cured Pork, 100
Pea, Sweet, Soup with Yogurt and Mint, 156
Peach, Tomato, and Basil Salad, 130
Pear
  Pecans, and Blue Cheese, Spinach Salad with, 133
  and Slow-Cooked Onions, Grilled Cheese with, 121
Pecans
  and Cheese, Maple Sweet Potatoes with, 167
  Pear, and Blue Cheese, Spinach Salad with, 133
  Tahini, Pomegranate, and Parsley, Roasted Eggplant with, 162
Peppers. *See also* Chile(s)
  Red Sofrito, 66–67
  Roasted Red, and Goat Cheese, Hash Browns with, 170
  Salsa Rossa, 84
  Sweet Potato Hash with Salsa Rossa and Sour Cream, 177
Pesto, Basil, Spaghetti with, 113
Pico de Gallo, 141
Pine Nuts
  Celery, and Cheese, Iceberg Salad with, 126
  Spaghetti with Basil Pesto, 113
Polenta
  Poached Egg, Pancetta, and Parmesan, 186

with Pork, Apples, and Slow-Roasted Onion, 111
  Soft, 76–77
Pomegranate
  -Parsley Salad, 216
  Tahini, Parsley, and Pecans, Roasted Eggplant with, 162
Pork. *See also* Bacon; Ham; Sausage
  Apples, and Slow-Roasted Onion, Polenta with, 111
  and Chile Chickpea Stew with or without Poached Eggs, 194
  Cuban Grilled Cheese, 125
  Cured, Pasta with Tomato and, 100
  and Kimchi, Fried Rice with, 114
  Poached Egg, Polenta, Pancetta, and Parmesan, 186
  Pozole, 211
  Shoulder, Slow-Roasted, 46–49
  Spaghetti and Meatballs, 96
  Tacos with Cabbage Slaw, 197
Potato(es). *See also* Potato Hash Browns; Sweet Potatoes
  and Chicken Salad with White Wine and Herbs, 123
  Creamy Mushroom Soup, 157
  Fingerling, with Green Garlic Vinaigrette, 168
  Kale, and Sausage Soup, Portuguese, 148
  and Leek Soup, 78–81
Potato Hash Browns, 32–34
  with Goat Cheese and Roasted Red Peppers, 170
  Mushrooms, and Warm Vinaigrette, Steak with, 182
  with Smoked Salmon and Things That Go with Smoked Salmon, 171
Pozole, Pork, 211
Purees, 78–81

R

Radishes, Pickled, and Soy Vinaigrette, Steak Salad with, 215
Raita, Cucumber, 86
Ramen, Gussied-Up Instant, 95
Rémoulade, 143
Rice
  Crisped, with Sausage and Kimchi, 103
  Foolproof, 40–41
  Fried, with Pork and Kimchi, 114
  Garlic-Soy Tofu Burritos, 141
  Lemon-Mint, and Salmon with Raita and Lettuces, 185

Louisiana-Style Dirty, with Greens, 99
  Savannah Red, 110

S

Saag Paneer, Kinda (Curry Spinach and Tofu), 173
Salads
  Chef's, 117
  Chicken and Potato, with White Wine and Herbs, 123
  Fennel and White Bean, 124
  Green, Classic, 28–29
  Iceberg, with Celery, Pine Nuts, and Cheese, 126
  Poached Egg and Bacon, 118
  Pomegranate-Parsley, 216
  Red Check, 129
  Roasted Chicken, 202
  Spinach, with Pear, Pecans, and Blue Cheese, 133
  Steak, with Green Papaya, 193
  Steak, with Pickled Radishes and Soy Vinaigrette, 215
  Three-Bean, 134
  Tomato, Peach, and Basil, 130
  Tomato-Crouton, 137
  Wheat Berry, with Tomato, Feta, Mint, and Olives, 107
Salmon
  and Lemon-Mint Rice with Raita and Lettuces, 185
  Pan-Roasted, 75
  Smoked, and Things That Go with Smoked Salmon, Hash Browns with, 171
Salsa
  Pico de Gallo, 141
  Rossa, 84
  Verde, 85
  Verde, Celery, 205
  Verde, Escarole, and Pickled Chiles, Rib-Eye Steak with, 207
  Verde, Tomatillo, 197
Salt, 16
Sandwiches
  Avocado Toast with Feta and Roasted Broccoli, 120
  Cuban Grilled Cheese, 125
  Fried Shrimp Po'boys, 142
  Grilled Cheese, 56–57
  Grilled Cheese with Pear and Slow-Cooked Onions, 121
  Grilled Cheese with Tomato, Ham, and Slow-Cooked Onions, 144
  Luxe Patty Melt with Slow-Roasted Onions and Pickles, 128
  Roasted Tofu and Bacon Club, 138

Sauces. *See also* Salsa
Cucumber Raita, 86
Nuoc Cham, 87
Rémoulade, 143
Special, 128
Super Simple, 82–87
Tahini, 162
Tomato, Back-Pocket, 52–53
Sausage
Kale, and Potato Soup,
Portuguese, 148
and Kimchi, Crisped Rice
with, 103
Shakshuka (Sweet Potato and Eggs
in Spicy Green Tomato Sauce),
158
Shallots, Pickled, Feta, and Mint,
Roasted Carrots with Tops
and, 161
Shellfish
Fried Shrimp Po'boys, 142
Spaghetti with Shrimp and Leeks,
104
Steamed Clams with Mushrooms,
Coconut Milk, and Chiles, 201
Steamed Mussels with Sofrito, 198
Shrimp
Fried, Po'boys, 142
and Leeks, Spaghetti with, 104
Slaw
Cabbage, Pork Tacos with, 197
Simple and Classic, 64–65
Sweet Onion, 191
Slice, defined, 19
Sofrito, Red, 66–67
Soups
Black Bean, with Avocado and
Sour Cream, 152
Butternut Squash and Apple, 147
Chicken, Italian, 151
Kale, Potato, and Sausage,
Portuguese, 148
Leek and Potato, 78–81
Mushroom, Creamy, 157
pureed, 78–81
Rich Tomato, with Bread, Basil,
and Olive Oil, 145
Sweet Pea, with Yogurt and Mint,
156
White Bean and Ham, Smoky, 155
Soy-Garlic Tofu, Slow-Roasted,
54–55
Spices, 15
Spinach
Italian Chicken Soup, 151
Salad with Pear, Pecans, and Blue
Cheese, 133
Strip Steak, and Onion Puree, 180
and Tofu, Curry, 173

Squash
Butternut, and Apple Soup, 147
Seared Summer, with Mint and
Vinaigrette, 174
Stews
Chicken and Dumplings, 204
Chicken Tortilla Chip, 212
Pork and Chile Chickpea, with or
without Poached Eggs, 194
Pork Pozole, 211
Sweet Potato(es)
Baked, 38–39
Hash with Salsa Rossa and Sour
Cream, 177
Maple, with Pecans and Cheese, 167
and Eggs in Spicy Green Tomato
Sauce, 158
with Tofu, Scallions, and Soy
Vinaigrette, 166
Swiss Chard, Garlic Sautéed, 63

T

Tacos, Pork, with Cabbage Slaw,
197
Tahini
Pomegranate, Parsley, and
Pecans, Roasted Eggplant
with, 162
Sauce, 162
Toast, Avocado, with Feta and
Roasted Broccoli, 120
Tofu
Burritos, Garlic-Soy, 141
Curry Spinach and, 173
Roasted, and Bacon Club
Sandwich, 138
Scallions, and Soy Vinaigrette,
Sweet Potatoes with, 166
Slow-Roasted Soy-Garlic, 54–55
Tomatillo Salsa Verde, 197
Tomato(es)
Chef's Salad, 117
Chicken Tortilla Chip Stew, 212
-Chile-Coconut Broth, Seared
Catfish with, 208
Corn, and Slow-Roasted Onion
Salad, Roasted Chicken with,
203
-Crouton Salad, 137
Feta, Mint, and Olives, Wheat
Berry Salad with, 107
Glaze and Sweet Onion Slaw,
Skillet Meatloaf with, 190
Ham, and Slow-Cooked Onions,
Grilled Cheese with, 144
Pasta with, and Cured Pork, 100
Peach, and Basil Salad, 130
Pico de Gallo, 141

Red Check Salad, 129
Red Sofrito, 66–67
Roasted Tofu and Bacon Club
Sandwich, 138
Salsa Rossa, 84
Sauce, Back-Pocket, 52–53
Sauce, Chickpeas, Ricotta, and
Basil, Cavatelli with, 108
Soup, Rich, with Bread, Basil, and
Olive Oil, 145
Spaghetti and Meatballs, 96
Spicy Green Sauce, and Sweet
Potato and Eggs in, 158
Sun-Dried, –Olive Vinaigrette,
Leeks in, 165
Tortilla Chip Chicken Stew, 212
Tortillas
Garlic-Soy Tofu Burritos, 141
Pork Tacos with Cabbage Slaw,
197

V

Vegetables. *See also specific
vegetables*
pureed, 78–81
Roasted, 60–61
Vinaigrette, Classic, 26–27

W

Wheat Berry Salad with Tomato,
Feta, Mint, and Olives, 107

Y

Yogurt
Cucumber Raita, 86
and Mint, Sweet Pea Soup with,
156

Published in the United States by Clarkson Potter/Publishers, an imprint of
Random House, a division of Penguin Random House LLC, New York.
clarksonpotter.com

CLARKSON POTTER is a trademark and POTTER with colophon
is a registered trademark of Penguin Random House LLC.

Library of Congress Cataloging-in-Publication Data

Names: Acheson, Hugh, author. | Lee, Andrew Thomas, other.
Title: How to cook: building blocks and 100 simple recipes for a lifetime of meals /
Hugh Acheson ; photographs by Andrew Thomas Lee.
Description: New York : Clarkson Potter, 2020. | Includes index.
Identifiers: LCCN 2019059560 (print) | LCCN 2019059561 (ebook) |
ISBN 9781984822307 (trade paperback) | ISBN 9781984822314 (ebook)
Subjects: LCSH: Cooking. | LCGFT: Cookbooks.
Classification: LCC TX714 .A376 2020 (print) | LCC TX714 (ebook) | DDC 641.5--dc23
LC record available at https://lccn.loc.gov/2019059560
LC ebook record available at https://lccn.loc.gov/2019059561

ISBN 978-1-984-82230-7
Ebook ISBN 978-1-984-82231-4

Printed in China

Design and hand lettering by Sonia Persad
Illustrations by Hugh Acheson
Photographs by Andrew Thomas Lee

10 9 8 7 6 5 4 3 2 1

First Edition